PENGUIN BOOKS
DEVLOK WITH DEVDUTT PATTANAIK

Devdutt Pattanaik is the author of over twenty-five books and 500
articles on the relevance of mythology in modern times. Trained in
medicine (MBBS from Grant Medical College, Mumbai University),
he worked in the healthcare and pharmaceutical industries for fifteen
years before devoting all his time to his passion for decoding beliefs
of all cultures, modern and ancient, located beneath the veneer of
rationality. To know more, visit devdutt.com

DEVLOK
with **Devdutt Pattanaik**

PENGUIN BOOKS

PENGUIN BOOKS

USA | Canada | UK | Ireland | Australia
New Zealand | India | South Africa | China

Penguin Books is part of the Penguin Random House group of companies
whose addresses can be found at global.penguinrandomhouse.com

Published by Penguin Books India Pvt. Ltd
7th Floor, Infinity Tower C, DLF Cyber City,
Gurgaon 122 002, Haryana, India

First published by Penguin Books India 2016

ISBN 9780143427421

Typeset in AJensonPro by Manipal Digital Systems, Manipal
Printed at Thomson Press India Ltd, New Delhi

www.penguinbooksindia.com

Contents

Author's Note

* This is a collection of easy-going conversations about Indian mythology, based on the eponymous television show
* What is discussed here is not meant to be factually 'accurate'—you may refer to your guru for clarity
* This is not an academic work and does not claim to be authoritative
* Contained here are simplified versions of mythological tales, taken from various versions found in different scriptures and in folklore
* The attempt is to retain the essence embedded in the tales, and to provoke readers to dig deeper into the philosophy
* I offer here a subjective truth, *my* truth, which is one among many truths, because:

> Within infinite myths lies an eternal truth
> Who knows it all?
> Varuna has but a thousand eyes
> Indra, a hundred
> You and I, only two

1

Holy Texts

There are many granths in Indian Puranic culture, like the Vedas, the Puranas, the Mahabharata and the Ramayana. Which was the first granth?

We should be careful when using the word 'granth', because granths, or what we call holy texts, came into existence only about 2000 years ago. Before that, there was the oral tradition alone.

The first Veda was the Rig Veda. Perhaps a little later came the Sama Veda and Yajur Veda. And then came the Atharva Veda. So, the Vedas are the first set of oral texts, which began to be transmitted to humans about 4000 years ago.

The Upanishads came 3000 years ago. They are actually explanations. The Ramayana, the Mahabharata and the Puranas were born 2000 years ago in Sanskrit.

Nearly 1000 years ago, poets started writing these in their local languages, resulting in texts such as the Kamban Ramayana in Tamil, the Balram Das Ramayana in Oriya, the

Eknath Ramayana in Marathi, the Ezhuthachan Ramayana in Malayalam.

Then we come into the modern age. The Tulsi Ramayana, which was written in Awadhi, is about 500 years old.

What are Upanishads?

Upanishad technically means sit down and talk to me, like a discussion or a chat. It involves inquiry on any subject; what we call mimansa. Specifically, the focus is on the atma—the soul, consciousness, essence, and so on.

The Vedas contain many mantras, detailed rituals and melodies. The Upanishads discuss at length the meaning, the mystery of the Vedas. They are commentaries that emerged out of discussions between rishis, kings, children, men and women, husbands and wives in an effort to unravel the meaning of the Vedas.

The Ramayana and the Mahabharata are in fact these meanings and secrets conveyed in the form of stories.

To sum up, the Vedas (4000 years old) were where ideas perhaps originated. The Upanishads (3000 years old) explained the meaning of the Vedas. The Puranas and the epics (2000 years old) expressed these ideas through stories.

So, Puranic stories have existed for many centuries. We've heard many stories in the form of geet, songs, many we saw as natak, drama. What came first? Were stories told through song or drama, or have both coexisted from the beginning?

The simple answer is that geet came first. The mantras from the Vedas were chanted. How this chanting was done—the pronunciation, the rhythm, the melody—was very important. The Sama Veda, in fact, focuses on melody, or music.

Gradually, when the Yajur Veda came into existence, these songs, the oral tradition, began to be associated with the rituals and ceremonies of the yagna. That means people started performing, and the yagna itself became an elaborate performance. There were characters with roles and specified lines to be chanted at specific points. Thereafter, people started telling and enacting stories between yagnas to keep others entertained. That's how natak, drama, began. It immediately gained so much popularity that it became hard to distinguish whether it was part of the yagna or just an interlude. The Natyashastra, the ancient treatise on drama, then became the Pancham Veda, the fifth Veda.

Although there are characters like Indra, Surya and other gods in the Vedas, there are no clear stories, only minor anecdotes here and there. It was in the age of the Puranas, 2000 years ago, when epic poems like the Ramayana and the Mahabharata were composed, that drama formally made its debut. Some say it was introduced by the Greeks who came to India with Alexander. Others say we adopted their practices and merged them with our own version of drama at that time. We draw this assumption from words like the Sanskrit Yavanika—literally, that which came from Greece—used to describe a stage curtain. It is significant that the famous Srinathji temples in Gujarat and Rajasthan have a Pichwai painting at the back, that functions essentially as a stage backdrop.

About 1000 years ago people began building temples with natyashalas, or theatre houses, inside, where plays adapted from the Ramayana and the Mahabharata would be performed. So along with song and dance, drama too was performed before the gods. The performance in the temples became very important. The theme of the plays would be the birth of Krishna or stories from the Ramayana. What used to be performed in royal courts was now staged in temples. The modern-day Kathakali, for example. With the arrival of the Mughals, however, drama gradually returned to the courts of kings.

The evolution of song and drama truly has a very interesting history.

Did the storytellers create these stories or did they hear them from somewhere? Where did these stories originate?

The word original is very dangerous. There is nothing original in Sanatan Dharma. Ideas come and go, and they return. Like cyclical waves, they rise and fall, and nothing can be termed original.

It is said that when the four Vedas emerged from Brahma's head, they were taken by the asuras and hidden in water. Then Vishnu, as Hayagriva, recovered them from the ocean. Hay means horse. Hayagriva had a human body but a horse's head. He searched for the Vedas in the water, and retrieved them after fighting the asuras. This is the story of something that is lost, then found, rediscovered, retold. Who then is the real source of the Vedas? They emerged from Brahma's head, so he can be seen as the originator, but Hayagriva searched and recovered them, so he too can be the source.

This conundrum exists in the storyteller's stories as well. Was the Ramayana Valmiki's creation or Narada's from whom Valmiki heard it? Or the crow Kakbhusandi's who narrated it to Narada? Or Shiva from whom the crow heard it? Why is it told like this? Because nobody knows who the original source is.

Likewise with the Mahabharata. Who knows the exact Mahabharata? Does Vyasa know it? There's a story where Jaimini goes to Vyasa seeking some answers to the Mahabharata. When he doesn't find Vyasa, he goes to his disciple Vaisampayan. But Vaisampayan has taken an oath of silence so he can't say anything. So what does Jaimini do? There are four birds who answer his questions—there, you have another route for the source. Is the Mahabharata that which Vyasa narrated to Ganesha? Or is it that which Vaisampayan told Janamejaya? Or what Romaharshan told Ugrasraiva after overhearing Vaisampayan?

There are always stories that complicate the issue of the source, and show that nothing is truly original; everything's come from somewhere. This concept of originality—of a beginning and an end—is very Western. Here, it is different. It's like searching for a corner in a circle—you'll never find it!

We've heard that Ved Vyasa was very intelligent, that he was a great organizer. What can you tell us about him?

Ved Vyasa was the composer of the Mahabharata. Vyasa means organizer, so Ved Vyasa is really the person who organized the Vedas. And the Puranas. The story goes that there was a severe famine that lasted twelve, fourteen or 100 years, depending on the version, when the Vedas got lost. That's when Vyasa found, collected and organized them in a particular format—the way we know them as the four Vedas. Ved was a fisherwoman's son. We tend to think of him as a Brahmin because that's how he's been portrayed. Caste, jati, became rigid about 2000 years ago.

When you read the Vedas . . . the problem, in fact, is that you can't *read* the Vedas; they're meant to be *heard*.

Just the way you can't read the Beatles—you've got to hear them!

There are ten books of Vedas called mandalas—a mandala is a circle, a concentric circle. Inside each mandala are poems called suktas. Within these are verses called rigs or richas. Verses turn into poems that make chapters, or mandalas. These mandalas are collected in a bundle called a samhita. So you have the Rig Samhita, Yajur Samhita, Sama Samhita, Atharva Samhita. This is what Ved Vyasa did—the original Excel sheet, if you will! So, the first verse of the first poem of the first mandala of the first samhita of the Rig Veda can be identified as Rig 1.1.1, all thanks to Ved Vyasa.

The Vedas are abstract—they're poetry, full of proverbs, allegory, symbols—and Vyasa thought ordinary people might not be able to understand them. So he composed the Puranas; Vyasa is associated with all the Puranas as well. He started conveying the essence of the Vedas in the form of stories. He was, of course, a great man.

Historically, Vyasa is 4000 years old and the Mahabharata and the Puranas are about 2000 years old. How long did Vyasa live then? More than 2000 years? Or do these stories simply connect the two works of literature by attributing them to one source—Ved Vyasa? We must be careful about reading the stories literally.

A historian may say that Vyasa was not one man but a tradition. Even today, a dais or a platform from where a teacher gives her lecture is called Vyasapeeth. Broadly, Vyasa could be a group of scholars or librarians who put together centuries of knowledge. I can't say whether he was a man or a woman, short or tall, dark or fair. We like these stories, but it was perhaps a tradition.

It is said that Rishi Valmiki wrote the Ramayana. But you say Narada did. So, who wrote the Ramayana—Rishi Valmiki or Narada?

It's interesting you use the word rishi for Valmiki. He was not a rishi; he was a poet, or kavi. Although we use these terms interchangeably, they mean different things. Valmiki was the Adi poet, the first composer of poetry. He was not a Brahmin but an ordinary man who had fallen on bad times, and was forced to steal to survive and support his family. Once, a sadhu he was stealing from asked him the reason he was doing so, and he said he was doing it for the sake of his family. The sadhu counselled him to ask his family whether they would share his bad karma, his sins, just as they were partaking of the loot. When he realized that his family was unwilling to do so, he took the advice of the sadhu and abandoned his criminal ways. He agreed to do penance, and the sadhu narrated to him the Rama katha, or the story of Rama. He then sat in meditation, reciting the name of Rama, and over time a termite hill formed around him. A termite hill is called val in Sanskrit, which means sand; that's where Valmiki's name is derived from.

So how did Valmiki turn into a poet from an ordinary poor man who used to be a thief? He'd heard Rama's story from the sage and had become wise. One day, as he was watching a pair of birds flying, a hunter's arrow suddenly struck the female bird and killed it. When he saw the agony of the male bird who was circling its dead mate, Valmiki cursed the hunter: 'May you suffer like the male bird. Your karma will haunt you.'

His words came out in rhyme, and sounded like poetry. So, his words that arose from grief, shoka, became the verse,

shloka. That is how poetry was born. Pleased with all these—
the poetry, the ideas, the thought of Rama—he decided to
compose an entire poem about Rama, the Ramayana.

The Ramayana is eternal, limitless—it has neither
beginning nor end. So, this is Valmiki—even the storyteller
has a story!

How does one access the original texts of the Vedas, Puranas and the Upanishads?

It may surprise you but all these are easily available online—
use your phone, computer, type 'sacred texts of India' in
Google and search them. We don't realize that there are
translations, original formats, scanned material from libraries,
etc., all accessible through the Internet.

Beginning with the Rig Veda, which was composed 4000
years ago, these texts existed only in the oral tradition until
about 2000 years ago. First these texts were recorded in the
Brahmi script, perhaps on leaves, in the time of King Ashoka.
Leaves get spoiled so they had to be rewritten, leaf by leaf;
this was done in ashrams, universities or in Brahmins' homes.
Later, they were written in the Sharada script and finally in
Devanagari. They were put on paper for the first time only
500–600 years ago.

Although we criticize the British, it is because of them that
the written texts, the granths, were brought into libraries from
which translations, commentaries, printed versions became
available. Libraries in India, the United States and Europe
have put all these on the Internet. As a result, many of our
original scriptures are widely available.

2

The Ramayana and the Mahabharata

In the 1980s two big TV shows were screened: *Ramayana* and *Mahabharata*. There was hardly any family in India that did not watch these shows. How did these epics become so important?

These two epics talk about family life. To understand their importance, we need to go back 2500 years in history to when Buddhism arose in India.

Buddha began to spread his philosophy, which propagated that all sorrows arise from desire; so to end sorrow, one must give up desire. The sanyas tradition, renunciation of material life, took root in a big way. When the value of everyday life, worldly life, started dwindling, the wise people of the time felt it would create an imbalance if everyone became a monk.

The poets, rishis, Brahmins of the time thought of ways to integrate spiritual values in everyday life. As a solution, they composed the Ramayana and the Mahabharata, which talk about family values. These epics are basically property disputes. The Ramayana is about whose son will ascend the throne and the Mahabharata is about a fight between cousins over Kurukshetra. The story of every family! Through Rama in the Ramayana and through Krishna in the Mahabharata, there is discussion over familial issues—how much is to be shared, what is one's own, what belongs to the other, and so on. These stories communicated the knowledge of the Vedas, and that's why they became so popular.

These stories came into being almost 2000 years ago and are said to have evolved over 400–500 years. In the period between the Maurya (2300 years ago) and Gupta (1700 years ago) dynasties, these texts were formalized in Sanskrit. Before this, they existed in the oral tradition, and emerged from different places. These stories may be much older. We don't know.

Which came first—the Ramayana or the Mahabharata?

There are different answers to this question. According to the Puranas, that is in mythology, there are four yugas: Krita, Treta, Dvapara and Kali.

The events in the Ramayana happened at the end of Treta and the beginning of Dvapara, while those in the Mahabharata happened at the end of Dvapara and beginning of Kali. So, in this scheme, the Ramayana came first. In Ved Vyasa's Mahabharata, Yudhishtira is told the story of the Ramayana as if it happened in the past. That is, Rama existed before Krishna.

In literary terms, it appears that the Mahabharata came first. That's because the Sanskrit in the Mahabharata is crude compared to the Ramayana. These stories were written over a period of 600 years, not by one writer in a month's time! And before that there was the 400-year-old oral tradition, so they've evolved over 1000 years. It's not easy to explain.

Anthropologists and sociologists would say that the polyandrous society in the Mahabharata seems more primitive than the monogamous one of the Ramayana, so the Mahabharata probably came first.

Historically as well, the Mahabharata talks of north India—the Kuru Panchaal area that is now Haryana, Delhi and Uttar Pradesh—whereas the Ramayana goes into the south so it probably came later.

In all this, where does Krishna's raas-leela feature—in the Ramayana or the Mahabharata?

Again, there's no single answer. Krishna's childhood stories, of cowherds, Gokul, Vrindavana, don't appear in the Mahabharata. Words like Govinda, Gopala do appear sometimes, but there are no stories about Yashoda, Devaki, and others. These appear in the *Harivamsa*. This story was written 1600 years ago and is mentioned in the Vishnu Purana, composed 1500 years ago. The Bhagavata Purana, that came 1000 years ago, describes Krishna's childhood in detail. Interestingly, Radha does not feature in it. The raas-leela is mentioned but Radha does not appear in it. She appears in Jayadev's *Gita Govinda* written 800 years ago. People say that in Prakrit poems the name Radha appears, or perhaps she is hidden somewhere in the Bhagavata Purana but there's no concrete proof. So Krishna's raas-leela was *written* about after the Ramayana and the Mahabharata, but, according to the story, it *took place* after the Ramayana and before the Mahabharata.

Amidst all this, where does our beloved Shiva appear, and when do his stories come?

The Ramayana, the Mahabharata and the Bhagavata Purana are all stories of Vishnu under the umbrella of the Vishnu Purana. Vishnu has many avatars that take mortal form, among whom Rama and Krishna are the most famous. These huge epics were written about them in the Vaishnava tradition. Parallel to this, the Shaiva tradition also developed.

The tree of Hinduism has two branches—the Vaishnava and Shaiva. The Vaishnava tradition is about participating in the world. In this, you have the monogamy of the Ramayana, the polyandry of the Mahabharata and Krishna's raas-leela. When Krishna marries, he takes many wives. So different worldviews, different traditions, but all within worldly existence. The Shaiva tradition is about withdrawing from the world. Shiva's stories are in the Shiva Purana, which is 1500–2000 years old, and was written around the time of the Ramayana and the Mahabharata.

Where is Shakti in all this? Where are her stories?

So, when these parallel branches arose, people asked of the Shaiva tradition, where is the Devi? Both the Ramayana and the Mahabharata have the Devi, but in the background. Likewise in the Shiva Purana. From the background, the Devi emerges into the foreground around 1200 years ago, just before the Bhagavata Purana. All these texts were in Sanskrit. The process of translating them into regional languages began 1000 years ago; English translations can be dated back to 100–200 years ago. This is how they evolved.

The Ramayana and the Mahabharata are known as itihas, history. Would it be correct to see them as actual historical events?

The word itihas, history, can be seen in two ways—spiritual and scientific. In the scientific view, there would have to be archaeological evidence, data, and so on, for something to be considered a fact. According to this, there is no epigraphical or archaeological data available for the Ramayana and the Mahabharata. Scientifically these would be called poetry, not fact.

However, spiritually, itihas is peoples' memory. People have been told: These are your memories. Memory and history are two different things. In pure philosophical terms, itihas means this is how life is. The Ramayana and the Mahabharata are a narrative device to teach philosophy.

Rama is a maryada purushottam, a man who follows rules and abides by religion. In the Mahabharata, Krishna is leela purshottam, a man who does not follow rules but abides by religion. So there are all kinds of people—those who follow rules and those who break them; those who abide by religion and those who don't—and how they exist with each other, through what relationship, is what the Ramayana and the Mahabharata explain.

Itihas means 'aisa hi hota tha, aisa hi hota hai, aisa hi hota rahega'—this is how it was, this is how it is, and this is how it will continue to be. Itihas means sanatan, timeless. As long as human beings exist, as long as their property issues exist, these problems will remain. So, itihas may be seen through science, spirituality or belief—take your pick!

How many Puranas do we have?

Technically, it is said that there are 108 Puranas, which include the major or Maha Puranas, the minor or Upa Puranas, the local or Sthal Puranas belonging to a particular village or temple. So there are many Puranas, but of the 108, the main ones are the Shiva, Vishnu, Brahma and Devi Puranas. The

Brahma Purana is a mix of the Shiva and Vishnu Puranas. And the Devi Purana too is an important one.

As you've said earlier, the Vishnu Purana is about worldly life and the Shiva Purana is about renunciation. What is the Devi Purana about—what it its theme?

If you want to turn a sanyasi into a householder, what will you do—get him married! And if a householder wishes to renounce the material world, he will essentially have to renounce women. The Devi Purana talks about the life of the householder— about the difference between nature and culture. When to partake of the householder's life or to take leave from it is the central conflict in Hinduism. So the relationship with Devi is important. For Vishnu, Devi is sometimes his mother (Renuka), or wife (Sita), or friend (Draupadi).

Shiva's relationship with Devi is simpler. He is a sanyasi who becomes a householder. When he marries Devi, he becomes Shiva Shankara, and when he is apart from her, he becomes Gauri Shankara; as a loving husband, he becomes Uma Maheshwara—basically he turns domestic.

When were the stories of the Ramayana and the Mahabharata first narrated, and in what form?

Again, historically, we don't know the answer. In the Puranas, however, it is said that Rama's two sons, Luv and Kush, first narrate the Ramayana to Rama. They grow up in the ashram of Valmiki who teaches them the Ramayana that he has composed. The boys then go and tell the story to Rama. When Rama hears it, he asks them whose story it is. They say, 'It is yours,' and he responds, 'No, the one you're narrating is better than mine.'

The Mahabharata is narrated two or three times. In the Naimisha forest, where rishis reside, a sage, Ugrasrava Sauti, arrives. Sauti means storyteller and the leader of those who are listening is called Shaunak. So Sauti tells Shaunak the story of the Mahabharata, and says, 'I heard the story from my father, Romaharshan.' When you hear something that enthralls you, it makes your hair stand on end. So the meaning of romaharsha is goosebumps—implying that Sauti's father was an exceptional storyteller! Ugrasrava means one with a bold voice; and it is he who first narrates the story of the Mahabharata. He heard it from his father who'd heard it from Vaisampayan who'd heard it from Ved Vyasa.

The story of the Bhagavata Purana is very interesting. Arjuna's son is Abhimanyu, and his son is Parikshit. Once, Parikshit is bitten by a snake called Takshak. As he is dying, he begins to weep, wondering why he must die, what mistake he committed, what the meaning of life is—basically he begins to suffer existential angst. At that time, Vyasa's son Sukamani comes to him. Suka means parrot; Sukamani parrots his father's words to Parikshit. He tells Parikshit stories from the Bhagavata Purana, about Krishna's life, his childhood, the raas-leela, and so on. Listening to these stories Parikshit calms down and loses his fear of death.

Tell us something about the Gita, which is a part of the Mahabharata.

When we say Gita, we usually mean the Bhagavad Gita, which is what Krishna narrates to Arjuna before the Kurukshetra war. But the Mahabharata has many Gitas. There is the Vyadh Gita told to Yudhishtira by the sage Markandeya, the Kama Gita told to Yudhishtira by Krishna and the Anu

Gita told to Arjuna by Krishna after the war, in which he repeats the entire Bhagavad Gita. Among the many Gitas, the Bhagavad Gita, knows as just 'Gita', is the famous one. It appears in the Bhishma Parva, an adhyaya, a section, which is the mid-point of the Mahabharata, from where things begin to change.

Can we say the Ramayana and the Mahabharata were written in Sanskrit?

Yes. But there's a difference between what's written and what's in our minds. For instance, we know of the Lakshmana-rekha, but it is absent in the Sanskrit version. What is in our memory, what we carry in our minds, is the loka Ramayana, that is, the one written in a regional language. There are a number of languages in our country; the south primarily has Tamil, Telugu, Kannada, Malayalam, and then there are Tulu, Konkani, Marathi, Gujarati, Bengali, Oriya, Assamese, and so on. The poets who wrote the Ramayana in regional languages did not translate from Sanskrit but retold the story according to local needs. Theirs is a *recreation*, not an exact translation. The Ramayana is not just a granth, a written text; it's a tradition.

In every language, there could be twenty, twenty-five or even 100 versions. Which means there could be 300, 500 or 1000 Ramayanas in India. Every time a mother tells her child the story, it is her version that's more important than Valmiki's. His can be called the original Ramayana, not the one by Tulsi or Vyasa. People don't commonly know this but there's a Vyasa Ramayana too. Within the Mahabharata, there is an adhyaya where Rishi Markandeya tells Yudhishtira the story of Rama. Having gambled away his kingdom,

Yudhishtira laments that because of the Kauravas he has to live out thirteen years of exile in the forest. So Markandeya tells him that Rama was exiled for fourteen years for no fault of his, but he never cried! This is called the Ramopakhyan.

Sanskrit itself has many Ramayanas—those by the playwrights Bhavabhuti, Bhasa, and by the famous poet Kalidasa (called *Raghuvamsa*). So even when you mention the Sanskrit Ramayana, it is difficult to say which one. For instance, the Lakshmana-rekha is not there in the Sanskrit version; it first appeared in the Bengali Krittivasi Ramayana in the fifteenth century. The Awadhi version came later, in the form of Tulsidas's Ramayana. It cannot be considered the Hindi version, because Hindi is a very recent language. If you see the history of the Ramayanas, you'll get a history of India. The Kamban Ramayana in the tenth century, Dandi Ramayana of Odisha in the sixteenth century, Krittivasi in the fifteenth century. Broadly, the plot is the same in all, but the details differ. Like the Lakshmana-rekha which wasn't there before. Or the episode in the Valmiki Ramayana where Ravana just comes and abducts Sita. There is also no elaborate Sita swayamvara in Valmiki's version either, as in a nautanki, a play; Rama simply lifts and breaks the bow and marries Sita.

The tradition of the Rama-leela nautanki is 400–500 years old. Earlier, various plays were performed. Buddhism also has a Ramayana where Buddha counsels Ravana to quit his wrong ways and renounce his desires. Jainism also has a Ramayana where Rama is called Padma, or lotus. This title is given to him because he is so beautiful.

3

The Trimurti

Please explain the concept of the Trimurti to us.

The Trimurti, Holy Trinity, comprises three gods: Brahma, Vishnu and Shiva. Brahma is the creator of the Brahmanda, or universe; Vishnu sustains the universe; and Shiva destroys it. One is the Generator, the other the Organizer and the third is the Destroyer—G-O-D. This logic seems sound in principle, but in reality, if you do some research in villages, you won't find temples of the Trimurti. You'll find the murtis, idols, of Shiva within the Shaiva tradition, of Vishnu within the Vaishnava tradition, and of Devi within the Shakta (from shakti) tradition. So, on the ground level, in a trimurti—set of three idols—you'll find Devi's idol instead of Brahma's.

So, no one worships Brahma, and there are no temples for him. How is that possible?

There are a few temples here and there, but they are the exceptions to prove the rule. There's one at Pushkar in

Rajasthan and another in Kumbakonam in Tamil Nadu, but there's no tradition of Brahma. There are stories to explain this, as well many historical and anthropological reasons for this. In Hinduism there are broadly two periods: the Vedic period from 4000 years ago until 2000 years back, and the Puranic for the next 2000 years. In the Vedic period it was mostly the gods of nature, the devas—Surya (sun), Chandra (moon), Indra, Agni (fire)—who were worshipped. The concept of God, like Shiva, Vishnu, Brahma, did not really exist. This came in the Puranic period.

In the Vedic period, yagnas were conducted, but there was no idol worship, nor any temples or stories. The yagna was a complicated ritual, performed by Brahmins, where no one else was allowed, and it was rather esoteric. Temples were different. There were a natya mandap or theatre hall, a bhoga mandap where food is served, rituals, gods and goddesses, festivals. There were idols of Shiva, Vishnu and his avatars, or of Devi, but not of Brahma, possibly because he was associated with the Vedic period, with the yagna. In the Puranic period, Vedic practices were abandoned and the agama parampara, or temple tradition, was embraced; perhaps due to this shift Brahma is not worshipped. This is the anthropological, historical reason. But there are a number of other stories about it too.

According to one story in the Vaishnava tradition, there was pralaya, chaos, while Vishnu was asleep. When he awoke, the universe was born. From his navel emerged a lotus in which sat Brahma. When Brahma first saw the world, he got scared and Vishnu reassured him. Now you cannot worship a frightened god. He should be the one who removes your fears. That's why we worship Vishnu, and not Brahma.

In the Shaiva tradition, the story goes that Brahma and Vishnu used to fight with each other about who should be worshipped. Brahma would argue that he had created the world, while Vishnu contended that he was the one who protected it. Once, when Brahma visited Vishnu, Vishnu did not even rise to greet him. This offended Brahma and a war of words ensued between them to determine who was greater. The argument escalated to the point of a real war. Shiva intervened, turning into an agni-stambh, a pillar of fire, between them. The pillar extended above the sky and beyond the depths of the earth; it had neither beginning nor end. It was decided that whoever found the end of that pillar would be the greater one. Immediately, Vishnu turned into a varaha, boar, and dove into the netherworld to reach the bottom of the pillar. Meanwhile, Brahma turned into a rajhans, swan, and flew into the sky to find the top of the pillar. Along the way, he came across a Ketaki pushp which was descending towards the earth. The Ketaki pushp told him that he'd fallen from the peak of the fire pillar. Brahma realized it would take him many yugas, aeons, to get there, so he treacherously convinced the Ketaki pushp to give false testimony. He asked him to tell Vishnu that he had reached the peak of the pillar and had brought the Ketaki pushp along with him as proof. Unfortunately for Brahma, Shiva got wind of this treachery and wanted to destroy him, but upon Brahma's pleading, he calmed down somewhat, and cursed him instead: 'Since you used falsehood to be worshipped, you'll never be worshipped by anyone.'

Another story comes from the Shakta tradition. Brahma was sitting at a yagna with his wife Savitri. She said, 'I'll be back from a bath, don't start the yagna until then.' So Brahma waited and waited. The muhurat, auspicious time, was passing by and he became impatient. He created another woman from a cow—Gayatri, seated her by his side and started the yagna.

When Savitri returned, she got very angry. She said, 'Couldn't you have waited a while longer? No one will worship such an impatient god.'

Why do we worship Shiva who is the destroyer when we don't worship Brahma, the creator?

Usually when we think of the word destroyer, it evokes something negative. We believe Shiva is the destroyer of evil, and that's why we worship him. But by that logic, Brahma and Vishnu would be creators and preservers of evil. So that logic doesn't hold. We have to understand *what* is being created, preserved and destroyed such that the destroyer, not the creator, is being worshipped. The Rig Veda says creation comes from icchha, desire. In India, Buddhism arose 2500 years ago, which made the very important point that it is desire that causes suffering. This is how Brahma, who was the creator, became associated with suffering. So, just as Brahma is the creator of desire and of suffering, Shiva became the destroyer of desire and of suffering.

The story goes that Brahma created the Brahmanda in the form of a desirable woman to whom he was sexually attracted; he became obsessed with his creation. When his obsession took on dangerous proportions, Shiva had to rein him in through yoga. The balancing force between bhoga, participating in desire, and yoga, the restraint of desire, is Vishnu. What Vishnu does is locate kama, desire, in the other—one should fulfil others' desires, not one's own. He doesn't kill desire, rather he simply relocates it. Because of this, the roles change. So, creation is of desire and of suffering; preserving is sustaining the desire of others and taking away their suffering;

and the destroyer eliminates the cause of suffering. Shiva destroys Kama, the god of desire, as well as Yama, death. He is both Kamantaka and Yamantaka, destroyer of desire and destroyer of death.

All these three gods have unique features. Tell us a little about the images of Brahma, Vishnu and Shiva.

Brahma looks like an old wise teacher or sage. He has the tools for performing a yagna in his hand: a kamandal or pot, a spoon to pour ghee, a samhita of a Veda, a granth. He is associated with the Brahmin caste. Vishnu, on the other hand, always looks regal—wearing a crown, silk clothes, chandan or sandalwood paste and a garland of flowers called vanamali. In his hand he holds a shankh or conch shell, a chakra or spinning disc, and a gada or mace. When in his Rama avatar, Vishnu holds a bow, and a bansuri or flute in the Krishna avatar. Shiva is completely different. His entire body is smeared with ash, and he is known as Digambara, someone who does not wear any clothes. But images show him wearing animal skin—gaja charma, elephant skin, or vyaga charma, tiger skin—and with dreadlocks.

Shiva is associated with natural things. Vishnu, however, wears artificial, manufactured things. You need a whole battalion of farmers, spinners, weavers, dyers, etc., to procure these things, which are associated with civilization. So we have Brahma who created civilization with yagna. To manage and sustain civilization there is a raja, Vishnu. The destroyer is a vairagi, a renouncer, and those are the clothes he wears. The way these three gods appear and all the symbols associated with them reflect the nature of life and society.

You'd earlier spoken of the Shakta tradition, and we've been discussing the Tridev, or three male gods. Where is Devi in all this?

In Hinduism, there is a fundamental principle that prakriti (nature) is eternal, and nature is thought to be a devi. That's the canvas. In this the human being arrives. When we talk about male gods, it refers to the human mind. Many stories about gods and goddesses are told to depict the relationship of the human mind with Devi. In the Shakta tradition, Devi has a twofold relationship with Brahma. In one form she is his mother, Kali, and in the other, his daughter, Gauri. Kali represents aranya, or forest, and Gauri represents sanskriti, or the domesticated space of the village, by extension, civilization. Brahma, then, is the son of the jungle and the father of civilization. But Brahma does not respect these relationships so he is not worshipped. With Shiva, Devi has a very different relationship—that of a wife. Shakti goes to Shiva as the goddess of nature, first as Sati, then as Parvati. She tempts Shiva, draws him towards the householder's life and gets him to participate in it. Her most unique relationship, however, is with Vishnu. If you see idols of Vishnu, you'll see Lakshmi and Saraswati with him. They're both his wives. When Vishnu is in the avatar of Rama, Devi becomes his wife, Sita. When he is Parashurama, she becomes Renuka, his mother. He doesn't have a fixed role; it keeps changing depending on what the Goddess needs. If the Goddess is Draupadi, Vishnu becomes Krishna, her friend, and helps her. If the Goddess is Radha, Vishnu becomes Krishna, her lover.

Brahma always wants to control and dominate the Goddess for his own benefit, bhoga, which is why he isn't worshipped. Shiva prefers yoga, but the Goddess offers him bhoga, attracts him towards life. Vishnu has a mutually benefiting relationship with Devi. This relationship is known as leela, in which he gives as well as receives pleasure, or bhoga, and both display restraint or yoga simultaneously. This is an interesting relationship. It is strange that Vishnu is also known as Purushottama, the Supreme Man, yet his form is always feminine. This is almost like saying that a supreme man is feminine!

I've heard a story where Shiva chops off Brahma's head. How can one god do that to another?

You should never take Puranic stories literally. They are always symbolic, and use metaphors to explain concepts. We can't have five hands, three heads, ten hands, etc. now can we? These are always pointing towards something. In the Puranas, Brahma has five heads. When he saw nature, he was so attracted by her beauty that he sprouted more heads just to savour her beauty. The fifth head is Brahma's ego; pride and arrogance about his own creation could be seen in all the heads. All the gods and goddesses, and living beings were dismayed to see this in their Pitamaha, creator. They wondered why he was behaving like that, why he was becoming so attached. All the gods and goddesses started crying. At the sound of their weeping, or rudan, Rudra, the ferocious avatar of Shiva, appeared and cut off Brahma's fifth head. From this Shiva came to be called Kapalika—the one who holds a head, kapal, in his hand. It is interesting to note that Brahma sits inside the lotus in Vishnu's navel and his fifth head is in Shiva's hand.

What learning do we get for our modern-day life from the story of the Trimurti?

In our lives too, we keep creating, sustaining, destroying. Take money, for example. We earn, save, spend. Brahma is the one who earns, brings in the money. Vishnu spends and invests it in the market, enabling exchange so that commerce flourishes. Shiva is someone who is not interested in money at all; his is the attitude of non-attachment, vairagya. On the other hand, Brahma's children are so interested in money that they hoard and fight over it, which is why no one worships Brahma or his children. The one who does business with the world, is involved with it, is Vishnu, so we worship him. When we grow old and wish to get rid of our desires, we can follow Shiva's example by renouncing money. Each of us has all these qualities, mostly Brahma's, but we shouldn't encourage those. We should harness Vishnu's qualities, so that Lakshmi, money, follows us. Towards the end of our life, we should become like Shiva; renounce the material world and move on.

4

Colour

If we look within our culture, we see colour everywhere. In temples, the clothes for gods and goddesses are bright and colourful; even their skin colour is prominent. What is the history of this, and why is colour such a big deal for us?

In Europe you'll see grey everywhere—grey buildings, black clothes, or white—they don't use colour much. There were two traditions in India: one was vairagya, the ascetic tradition, which used simple colours; the other, grihastha, the householder's tradition, where colour was given a lot of importance. Colours signified well-being, prosperity, good luck. Perhaps when we saw the rainbow we believed that colours must have originated from there, in the gods' abode. And so colours became very important for us. Vishnu is known as Rangnath, the god of colour; Vaikuntha, the heavenly abode, is Rangabhoomi, the ground where colour is born; the world is a Rangamanch, a stage. So, life is a stage on which God's leela is played out. Enjoyment has different shades; just as food has different flavours, colour too has its spectrum.

There's a practical reason for this as well. India had been famous for its textile industry since ancient times, until it was destroyed by the British. This is why indigenously produced khadi became so important. We used to make cloth, but there was something special in what we did. Our secret was 'fixing' the colours on to the cloth. Only India made these colour fixers. Perhaps colourful cloth was found nowhere else in the world, be it in Arab or in European countries; that was unique to us. And if we gave colourful cloth to the whole world, we'd naturally give it to our gods too! Anywhere you go, even in South East Asia, you will hear that they want Indian textiles. Our textiles are as valuable as gold. Indians, in fact, traded textiles in exchange for gold. Before British rule, trade in colourful textiles was extremely significant. This is perhaps why, during ancient times, in our Puranic stories, in myths about gods and goddesses, we give so much importance to colour.

We have an obsession with light skin, as seen in the numerous fairness products in the market. But our gods— like Krishna—are dark-skinned. Was Krishna actually dark- or blue-skinned, and why is his dark colour important?

In every agrarian society, complexion is significant. Even in China, this divide exists. The presumption is that rich people don't step out of the house to work in the fields, are not exposed to the sun and do not get sunburnt or tanned. So, complexion is an indication of a person's class. There's a word, asuryasparsha, for a girl who's never been touched by the sun, meaning her skin is very light. This colour prejudice is found in all agricultural communities, not just in India. In India, many foreign invaders, who were fair, came from the north, so fairness is associated with power and wealth.

In the Puranas, however, all this is not relevant. There, colour is a spiritual matter and fairness and darkness have a completely different meaning. In the Indian subcontinent, the most exciting time is probably the advent of monsoon. We're an agrarian society and we get very excited when we see dark, heavy clouds, and peacocks dancing in the forests. The dark clouds—ghana-shyama—of monsoon and the joy they bring are associated with Krishna. Dark complexion is also associated with the dark, fecund earth, or dark tamarind forests—all this represents rich, fertile land.

Black is always paired with white. Shiva stays in the white snows of the Himalayas and is called Karpura Gauranga, one who is white as camphor. Vishnu is dark and Shiva is fair. There must be a contrast.

You might ask: Isn't Shiva dark, as depicted in pictures? In art, purple is actually the colour of ash, of grey objects. Since Shiva is an ascetic, he is smeared with ash. But in poetry or in literature he is called Karpura Gauranga.

To come back to the idea of contrast—Vishnu is dark, Shiva is fair; Krishna is dark, Balarama is fair; Radha is fair, Krishna is dark; Gauri is white, Kali is black; Yamuna is known as Kalindi, black, while Ganga is white. This contrast appears repeatedly to show that one complements the other. In Baul kathas, stories told by Bauls, itinerant singers of Bengal, the white Shiva is with Parvati who takes the dark form of Kali. After a while, Kali says, 'I'll take another form, I'll become Krishna,' and Shiva says, 'I'll become Radha.' So they change genders but retain their colour and the contrast between them.

These colours denote the two margas, paths, which exist in Puranic stories. White is the nivritti marga, that of vairagya, withdrawing from society, whereas black is the pravritti marga, of grihastha life, engaging with society. Krishna takes the pravritti marga, while Shiva takes the nivritti marga. In physics, black is said to absorb light whereas white reflects it— so again, there's an opposition. Rang or colour is a metaphor to show that the deities complement each other.

Paintings depict Krishna in blue. What does that mean?

Like Shiva was coloured purple to show ash, indigo, or neel, was used to show dark complexion. When you paint it on paper, it appears black; blue is the lighter version. Gradually, Krishna began to be painted blue. In our country, we don't like black—we prefer the unnatural blue over the natural black. It is rationalized by explanations like he has the colour of the sky, of ether; it is called blue-black instead of wholly black! The colour prejudice prevails; who knows when it'll disappear?

We know Lakshmi and Durga wear bold red saris, while Saraswati wears white. Are there any stories behind this?

There is always a story or an idea behind colours that illustrates a philosophy. Saraswati is associated with education, with simplicity. She wears a white sari, a plain fabric which cannot be dyed. Sometimes she wears yellow, particularly during Basant, or spring, when she is worshipped. This is because the flower of sarson, mustard seed, is yellow. Lakshmi is associated with the colour of earth. The soil is red before the monsoon, when it is ploughed. After the rains it becomes green. So Durga wears red before the rains, when she is depicted as a kumari, virgin, and green afterwards, when she becomes a mata, mother. In Mumbai, during Gauri puja— Gauri is Ganesha's mother—she is dressed in green. Red is also associated with power. As red is the colour of blood, it is the colour of shakti, that is, strength. Through these different stories, clothes and symbols, our subconscious mind is allowed to absorb different aspects of life and ideas.

While we're talking of colours, we must talk about Holi and how it started.

There is a story about it. Krishna, as a child, runs to his mother Yashoda and asks her why she made him black, while Radha is fair—why this injustice? Yashoda rubs turmeric paste on his cheek and sends him off, saying now his colour has changed. He brings kala jamun fruit for Radha and asks her to close her eyes so he can feed her. Instead, he rubs its dark juice on her skin and declares that she too is now dark.

The other colour that is really important in our culture is saffron, kesar. Priests wear saffron, Hanuman's colour is saffron, and kesar is always used on auspicious occasions. What is the significance of this colour?

Kesar, also known as bhagwa, appears in our country's flag. These days it is associated with Hinduism. In history, Hinduism was linked with red, called rakt chandan. The idols of Ganesha and Hanuman in Varanasi are red. Over time these have become orange. Historians and poets wanted to find out where this orange came from, because it's a colour that is usually associated with the monastic order. To reiterate, Hinduism has two traditions—one ascetic, the other of everyday life. Householders wear all colours, and red particularly is very important; as are yellow, blue, green, white. The significance of saffron suddenly increased perhaps because the world of the sanyasis, mahants and their maths gained in power over the last 1000 years. We began to assume that they were our only gurus, which wasn't the case earlier. We've had gurus who were married, women gurus, gurus from different castes, and so on, in our tradition. Somewhere, Hinduism began to be associated more and more with sanyas, renunciation, perhaps even with Buddhism. Their gerua colour, similar to brown, was very important; this slowly became a deeper orange and then saffron.

Saffron is also the tiger's colour and represents power. During the freedom struggle, Lokmanya Tilak gave it importance. Kesari also means tiger, and it is linked with strength and virility. So, saffron is associated with asceticism as well as masculinity. There's another possible reason: haldi, turmeric, and kumkum, red pigment, are often used in pujas. On mixing, you get orange. Perhaps red was too strong, and to soften it, haldi was mixed in it to give the colour of kesar.

Most of the bachelor gods, like Hanuman, wear saffron, but never Krishna, who wears pitambar, or yellow clothes. So, while it is primarily associated with asceticism and masculinity, in modern times saffron has also come to be identified with Hinduism.

Black is considered ashubh, inauspicious, in our culture. But Ayyappa worshippers in south India wear black; we worship Kali.

In Hinduism, nothing is fixed and unchanging. Things change with history, with geography—what happens in the north, does not in the south; what happens in the east, does not in the west. When we say in our dharma that a particular colour is inauspicious, it is true only for a certain community or region, not for the entire nation. India is a huge country, just as Hinduism is a vast religion; because of incomplete knowledge we feel what happens in our houses, our community holds true for all Hindus, but that's not how it is.

The colour black is associated with black magic, but it is also used in proper pujas. Special pujas use black a lot, like on someone's untimely death. Those familiar with agam literature will know that shubh–ashubh vary with region. It is difficult to know why the Ayyappans of Kerala wear black. We can speculate on the reasons. There are many Muslims and Hindus in Kerala. People who went to Haj wore white, so Ayyappans may have said, 'We'll wear black'. Another possibility might be that because people of all castes visit Ayyappa temples, and Brahmins wear white, the devotees chose black.

No colour is auspicious or inauspicious by itself—it depends on the situation. As they say in Ayurveda, there is no good or bad dosh, humour, as such. Only when the proportion goes haywire does it cause a problem. In Hinduism too there's nothing absolutely bad or good. Otherwise, we'd have to dye our hair white! In the *Gita Govinda*, there's a famous line in which Radha is mad at Krishna and says, 'I don't ever want to see black'; she wants to dye her hair and eyebrows white, and not go out at night, and so on. Her friend says, 'But when you close your eyes, you'll see only black. How can you run away from black?'

5

Shiva

Shiva is an integral part of the Trimurti. His persona is very dramatic. What can you tell us about Shiva's history?

Shiva's history goes back to the Vedas. In the Vedas, Indra, Surya, Agni, Vayu feature often; but there's not much mention of the gods we know today, like Shiva and Vishnu. However, Shiva finds mention as Rudra, his earlier name. There are many hymns to Rudra, like the Rudra stuti and the Rudra stotra, and it's as though the kavi, poet, is writing about Rudra with fear. It's said that Shiva was probably worshipped even in the Indus Valley civilization because seals depicting Shiva have been found. The seals show a seated yogi with a trishul, or trident, in his hand. In the Vedas there's no word like Shiva or Shakti, but there is Rudra. He's associated with vanaspati, jungles, animals, herbs, night. Rudra evokes fear, awe—as though he's some distant god whose name cannot be uttered. Atreya Brahmins say you shouldn't take his name before a yagna, only afterwards. He seems to be a very powerful deity, but you don't find stories about him, except in the Puranas that came after Buddhism.

These stories talk a lot about Shiva's wedding, which is curious. That's because the Puranic era was preceded by the Buddhist period, which was overarchingly about vairagya, or asceticism. Puranic stories—the Ramayana, the Mahabharata, the Shiva Purana—focused on family stories where importance was given to grihastha, the householder's, life. Basically, we see the characters from the Vedic period assume new domestic roles in Puranic stories. There's a clear tension between the material life and the ascetic path.

After this, around 2000 years ago, Shiva's temples began to be built—Kailasa at Ellora, the Brihadeshwara temple at Thanjavur, Tamil Nadu, and the Ekampara temple in Odisha. Another 1000 years later even bigger Shiva temples came up, proving that he'd become a popular deity. Thereafter the Shaiva math came into being, rivalling Vaishnava and Shakta maths. Like the Iyer–Aiyengar rivalry in Tamil Nadu, Shaivas and Vaishnavas used to compete for supremacy throughout India. Shiva has gained this importance over the last 2000 years. The first reference to him appeared perhaps in the Indus Valley civilization where he found mention as a distant god in the Vedas. It was in the Puranas that he acquired the status we associate with him today. It is there that we find the macho image of him we're familiar with— ash-smeared, draped in elephant or tiger skin, and with serpents coiled around him.

In many stories, Shiva is a sanyasi, ascetic, while in others he's a householder. You say he's both, but who is the real Shiva?

For this, you have to turn to Buddhist literature. The story goes that Siddhartha Gautam was a prince in the city of

Kapilavastu, and he had a wife and a child. Although he had everything, he was unhappy—he feared disease, old age, death, and wanted freedom from suffering. He left his home, took sanyasa, did tapasya, intense meditation, and realized that kama, desire, is the root cause of suffering.

In the Shiva Purana, the story is the other way round. Shiva is a yogi, a sanyasi, living in the Himalayas. Devi goes to him and says you must marry. She brings him down from Kailasa and marries him. So the ascetic becomes a householder. The movements in the two stories are opposite, and both these forms are important.

There's a tension here. He's moving towards yoga, or renunciation, while Devi is trying to draw him towards bhoga, or partaking in the world. After the wedding, he is completely transformed. He starts playing the veena, so is named Veenapani; dances, hence the name Nataraja; or tells stories to his wife. In the Ramayana and the Mahabharata, Shiva narrates stories to Shakti. In the Tantra-shastra, Parvati poses a question to him, which he answers. So, he becomes a storyteller, a scholar—earlier he was sombre, kept his eyes closed, but now he talks, discusses. Devi gets him to engage with the world. Shiva is the one who has withdrawn from the world, while Shankara participates in the world. These are the two forms that emerge in the Puranas.

Vishnu has avatars like Rama and Krishna. Why does Shiva have roops, or manifestations, and not avatars?

Shiva does have different forms, but they're of a different kind. Shiva comes to the samsara, the world, from vairagya, and Vishnu, while staying in the samsara, comes to

Bhu-loka, where he experiences birth and death. The form that experiences this, like a mortal, is called an avatar, and his descent from Vaikuntha, his heavenly abode, is avataran, transformation.

Shiva's stories don't have a connection with time, with birth or death. He is beyond this, so he has different roops. There's his Bholenath roop in north India—literally, the innocent one, someone who does not understand the ways of the world. When Ravana comes and sings a song for him, Shiva is pleased and asks him what he wants. Ravana says, 'I want your wife to become my wife,' and Bholenath agrees. He is so innocent that he doesn't even understand what a patni, a wife, means. Parvati realizes she has to handle the situation herself!

Another is the Bhairava roop, someone who's extremely short-tempered. At the smallest provocation, he gets angry and grows sharp claws, his eyes become bloodshot, and dogs and bhoots, ghosts, gather around him. From bhay, fear, comes bhairav, so basically he assumes a frightening, bhayanak roop.

Asutosh is another roop. Someone who's quick to lose his temper and quick to calm down. He'll get angry in no time, but if you ask for forgiveness, it will be granted immediately.

There's Ardhanareshwara, who is half-woman. He loves his wife so much that he offers her half his body so that they may always be together.

Interestingly, some pictures depict Shiva as a vairagi but along with Shakti and their children, which shows him to be an ascetic and a householder both. Just as we have various moods, emotions, and we change according to the situation, God too changes and has many roops. Broadly, he is a yogi who is converted to a bhogi by Devi.

While the temples to Rama, Krishna and other gods house their idols, Shiva's temples do not have his idol. Why is that so?

The Vedas were trying to convey something through the mantras and yagnas. They were followed by the Upanishads, which tried to extract the meaning of the Vedas; this resulted in Vedanta, or the end of the Vedas. In the Upanishads, the atma, or soul, acquires importance, and it is asked, 'What is the roop of atma?' The atma is formless, so how does one worship it? This has been given the shape of a Shiva-linga, which is a form of the atma. The puzzle here is how does one turn the nirgun, the formless, into sagun, one with form—that is why the Shiva-linga is placed in Shiva temples.

What is the story behind the Ganga flowing from Shiva's tresses?

Ganga is a river, that is asthir, continuously changing, moving, flowing. Shiva sits on a solid, immovable, unchanging mountain, which is sthir. These are two contrasting concepts. The still mountain is atma and the river is prakriti, nature, and the dialogue between atma and prakriti is the conversation between Shiva and Shakti.

The story goes that King Sagar loses all his sons to death. He wonders whether they'll be reborn. Kapila Muni tells Bhagirath, Sagar's grandson, that if the Ganga descends to the earth, Bhu-loka, from heaven, Swarga-loka, and if he immerses his father's and uncles' ashes in her waters, then they'll surely be reborn. Bhagirath performs intense tapasya to please Indra, and asks him to convince Ganga to descend to Bhu-loka. Ganga consents but says the force of her descent might destroy the world. Brahma asks her to go to Shiva since he is sthir, and what is stable can control that which is asthir. Shiva says, 'I'll sit in one place and Ganga can fall on my head.' Ganga laughs: 'His skull will split.' Shiva says, 'Let's see.' Ganga lands on Shiva's head and gets trapped in his dreadlocks. Her violent force is restrained, calmed, and she starts flowing like a regular river towards civilization.

The water falling from a hanging pot on to a Shiva-linga in Shiva temples symbolizes the Ganga. Shiva is a vairagi, in meditation, away from the world. Unless he is involved with the world, its problems cannot be solved. That is, the atma must be awakened. As I'd mentioned, in the Shiva Purana, Devi gets him to marry her—it is simply a way of getting him to engage with the world. Shiva either sits in deep meditation or, some say, he's high on bhang, cannabis, and is lost to the world. In Shiva temples, devotees also clap loudly to get him to listen. The yoni around the Shiva-linga is a roop of his wife who holds him tightly to this world, lest he run away. So his wife Gauri is holding on to him, Ganga is falling on his head, and devotees are clapping—all this is to awaken him.

Shiva temples can be anywhere—under a tree, at a cremation ground—unlike temples to Krishna, Vishnu or Rama, which have vaibhav, a form of Vishnu, in them. No special treatment or adornment is required in a Shiva temple. The simple Shiva-linga, with the Ganga above him, and the yoni beneath him are enough—you can throw bel leaves there, dogs can roam around, there is no issue. He's Bholenath, a simple god who demands little. Raw, unprocessed milk is poured on him, unlike other gods to whom butter or ghee is offered. These days, of course, some people have made it a business to have elaborate rituals for him. But Shiva is a guileless, direct, god—quick to get furious, quick to calm down;

he consumes bhang and remains mast, lost unto himself. He is a very different kind of god, doesn't distinguish between devas and asuras. He loves them all. His devotees include Ravana, Rama and Hanuman. Some say Hanuman is Shiva's swaroop.

When does Shiva use his third eye?

There's a famous episode in which Parvati goes to Shiva and wants him to look at her, but he is meditating and not interested. He's been through a traumatic experience: Sati, his wife, set herself on fire. An angry Shiva wrecked Daksha's yagna and withdrew from the world, retreating into his cave. When Parvati approaches him and he doesn't respond, Indra decides to intervene and make things exciting. He goes to Kama, the god of lust and desire, and asks him to shoot an arrow at Shiva. Kama arrives with vasant ritu, the season of spring, his apsaras in tow, and loosens an arrow. Shiva keeps his eyes closed but opens his third eye and reduces Kama to ash and smears the ash on himself. It's a terrifying aspect of Shiva. The third eye signifies destroying your own desires, which means annihilating life. Because life arises out of desire. Thus Shiva is known as the destroyer, a destroyer of desire.

The Shakta tradition has a different story, which believes that the third eye opened because of Devi. When Parvati appears before him, he sees how beautiful she is and realizes that two eyes will not be enough to take in her loveliness, so a third eye emerges to fully experience her beauty.

The first story is written in Sanskrit in the Puranas, the latter is not found in any text. It comes through the oral tradition. The Bauls of Bengal give Shiva's third eye, which is actually a weapon, a romantic aspect through this story of the Shakta tradition.

6

Jeev and Jantu

Where did the humans, devas, asuras and nagas that populate the Brahmanda, the universe, come from?

They are all Brahma's grandchildren. It is said that prakriti always existed, but the living creatures, jeev–jantus, came from Brahma. Brahma had many Manasputras, those born of the mind. In some stories they are Sapta Rishis (seven sages) or ten Prajapatis (ten patriarchs or fathers). Brahma also created women from his mind, though in some versions he is said to have created them from his body, and the rishis from his mind. He gave each rishi a wife from whom different kinds of jeev–jantu were born. For instance, Rishi Kashyapa had two wives, Diti and Aditi. On Aditi, he sired the Adityas (devas) and on Diti the Daityas (asuras). He fathered other creatures with his other wives: Vinata gave birth to Garuda (mythical human-eagle) and other birds; Kadru to nagas (serpents); and Surasa to reptiles. All these creatures, various birds, animals, yakshas—they are children of Brahma's son Kashyapa.

This is how a lineage is formed—the father is always the same—Kashyapa or, sometimes, Brahma himself—but the mothers are different. The body, flesh, comes from the mother, the mind from the father, so the characteristics of the children vary.

What are the qualities of the different jeev–jantus in the Brahmanda?

The devas live an entitled, lavish, leisurely life, like stars. They enjoy a rich, pleasure-filled existence, where they watch apsaras dance, gandharvas make music, and so on. If you call them for a yagna, they won't come unless you offer them a gift. But when they do come, they'll gift you something.

The perception of asuras differs. The devas perceive them as a threat because they feel the asuras jealously eye their wealth and are their rivals. Asuras, on the other hand, believe that the devas have wrongly seized the wealth they had created together, and hence think of themselves as the oppressed ones. Rakshasas are those who snatch and steal others' possessions, like Ravana stole Kubera's kingdom, Rama's wife Sita, etc. Yakshas are associated with hoarding they collect endlessly and build a treasure, which they never share with anyone. They are depicted as short, deformed beings, surrounded by beautiful women wearing precious jewels and gems—these women are part of the 'collection' of the miserly yakshas.

Devas are depicted as handsome, asuras as ugly. Rakshasas are shown to be powerful, while yakshas are deformed. The most beautiful beings are of course the gandharvas, musicians, born from gandha, the aroma of flowers. Apsaras are equally beautiful. Apsa means water, so they are like water; that's their essence.

Nagas are associated with fertility and are said to have magical powers. They are sexy, fearsome in a way, alluring. A Nagin is like a vishakanya, poisonous woman—she will attract you, but if she entraps you, she can destroy you as well.

If devas come from Swarga, heaven, where do asuras and rakshasas come from?

The Brahmanda is like a multi-storeyed building. What is above dharti, earth, is loka and below is tal. So devas live above the ground and asuras below in Patala. The word Patala comes from pa-talam, below the feet. Some say that asuras, yakshas, nagas, etc., find their origin not in the Vedas but in the non-Vedic tradition, perhaps from local clans and tribes. In Hinduism, one stream of thought came from the Vedas. Asuras are from the Vedas, but there they are equal to gods. Asuras become villains in the Puranas and they are banished under the earth. In the Gita, they live in Naraka, hell. So, you see, their status shifts. Devas, Devis, asuras, nagas, yakshas, all came from various periods and communities, and assembled in the stories in the Puranas.

Unravel the mystery of the Amrita manthan story for us.

Everybody fears death. But the gods possess something with which they can conquer death; it makes them amar, immortal. From the Vedas to the Puranas this concept gains in importance. There is an ocean of milk, Kshir Sagar, where the Amrita is hidden. The oldest story about Amrita manthan is not about Amrita at all, though. According to it, Lakshmi resides in this Kshir Sagar. Once, the affluent Indra insults Rishi Durvasa by ignoring him. Angered,

Durvasa curses him that he will lose all his wealth and well-being. He will also lose his shri, that is, luck and prosperity. This curse comes true and Lakshmi leaves heaven and hides in the Kshir Sagar. The devas are upset and want to draw her out from there. But they don't have enough power, so they take the asuras' help. Normally, in stories, devas and asuras are always fighting with each other, but this time they collaborate and churn the ocean—manthan. It may look like it, but it is very different from a tug-of-war, in which only one party can win. Here, when one pulls, the other lets go, and vice versa. Force and counterforce are used to achieve results. The idea is that if you cooperate when you churn, you can get butter, Lakshmi, maybe even Amrita—but not by arguing. Similarly, when two countries are at loggerheads with each other, neither will be able to get butter, that is, prosperity.

A philosophy emerges. Many objects and creatures emerge from the churning, and each one has its own significance. For instance, purusharth, the goals of life, comprises dharma, artha and kama. Their symbols emerge from Amrita manthan. The signs of dharma, duty, are the elephant, the horse; the signs of artha, materiality, are the Parijata tree, Kamadhenu cow, the Chintamani jewel; the signs of kama, desire, are the romantic moonlight, apsaras, and varuni, alcohol. All these emerge from Amrita manthan and are part of samsaric jeevan, worldly life. The chanting of Amrita manthan is also done during weddings, to wish for the couple's home to be filled with dharma, artha and kama. There is no moksha, liberation from the world, in Amrita manthan because it's about vairagya, sanyas. These are the symbols of the material—grihastha—life that results when devas and asuras cooperate.

Finally Amrita emerges. But along with it also comes poison. This suggests that whenever you draw something from nature, toxins are also produced. The idea is that nature is bountiful but needs to be used with care, its pollutants, toxins need to be handled as well. There are so many ideas that emerge from this one story.

Why are nagas worshipped?

Naga is an interesting concept in the Puranas. Nagas are always at war with Garuda. Nagas crawl on the ground, while Garuda is in flight, suggesting a conflict between the creatures on the ground and those in the sky. Nagas are always below the earth—Rasa Sthal, the land of rasa (literally, juice), where they say there are treasures, jewels. Naga-loka or Rasa Sthal is always associated with wealth. Ulupi, in the Mahabharata, possesses the powerful nagamani which cures all. This land is also associated with fertility. Nagas are believed to have rejuvenating powers, perhaps because they shed their skin and acquire a new one, and never grow old. Naga puja is done for fertility—for children, wealth, a good harvest, all of which are related to the material world.

Are yakshas, rakshasas and asuras the same?

In comic strips, all these are shown as dark beings, but they are different. Asuras are always fighting with devas; devas reside in Swarga, asuras in Patala. Rakshasas fight with humans, for example, the war between Rama, the king of human beings, and Ravana, the king of rakshasas. This war takes place on Bhu-loka. Rakshasas are always found in jungles; they are known as barbarians. In the Ramayana,

Ravana and Kubera, the king of yakshas, are brothers and both are children of Vishrava. Like Kashyapa, Vishrava was one of Brahma's sons. He had two wives; from one wife were born the rakshasas and from the other, the yakshas. Similar to devas and asuras, nagas and Garuda, rakshasas and yakshas are always at war. Yakshas had created and stored the wealth of Lanka, in the south, but the rakshasas came and seized it, pushing them to the north. Alanka, or Alaka, is in the north. Mount Kailasa houses the yakshas, while Lanka houses the rakshasas.

This may have astrological significance, or something to do with the sacred geography of the Puranic bhugol, the globe. It signifies that every force has a counterforce—devas–asuras, Garuda–nagas, rakshasas–yakshas. This is a recurring theme in the Puranas. This tension exists to create balance. The larger idea being that if there's ever a tug-of-war, it'll result in violence, but if there's a manthan, there will be collaboration which will lead to productivity.

Rahu and Ketu are asuras, yet we worship them—why?

The story goes that in Amrita manthan, an asura drank the Amrita, so Vishnu chopped off his head. The head became Rahu, the demon of eclipse, and the body became Ketu, a directionless comet, signifying restless energy. So why do we worship this negative energy? In yagnas, both sura or devas, and asura are invoked. This whole idea about devas being purely good and asuras being only evil is a recent one. Yes, they are enemies, but in terms of opposition, not morality or ethics. Traditionally, both are worshipped since they are force and counterforce in Amrita manthan. In the world too there are forces you may not like, but they are necessary. The value of the positive is enhanced by the presence of the negative. Both positive and negative forces are worshipped in Hinduism.

There may even be a murti, idol, of Ravana who's a rakshasa, in a Shiva temple. You can worship all the creatures, be they asuras, rakshasas, nagas, yakshas, plants or stone—it's about how much you can handle, how big-hearted you are. The idea is to include everyone. We worship goddesses like Shitala Maa (associated with smallpox), Jari Mari (associated with cholera)—we worship these goddesses of disease, pay them our respect while pleading with them not to visit our homes.

Tell us the story of Jaya and Vijaya, and how they were cursed to be born on earth.

The story is that four of Brahma's Manasputras go to visit Vishnu, but are stopped at the gate and told that they cannot enter and disturb a sleeping Vishnu. Enraged, they curse the gatekeepers that they will have to take birth on Bhu-loka three times—first as asuras, then as rakshasas and finally, as human beings. The gatekeepers—Jaya and Vijaya—go to Vishnu and ask him to lift the curse since they were only doing their duty. Vishnu expresses his inability to do so and says that they will have to be reborn on earth, but promises not to abandon them; their death on earth will always be at the hands of one of his avatars.

In the concept of rebirth, depending on your punya, the blessings you've accumulated, you can be reborn as a deva, asura, yaksha, any creature, even pishachas, ghosts. It signifies that we are related to and connected with all living beings. A being you look down upon as an animal in this birth may've been your brother or mother in a previous birth. The phrase 'Vasudeva Kutumbakam', the world is a family, is often used for travel shows these days, but it encompasses the concepts of inclusion and interconnectedness.

7

Indra

Indra is considered the king of devas, but he is not worshipped like the Trimurti. Why?

Hindu religion is considered sanatan, eternal, but historically it is only 4000 years old, when the Vedas were composed. Indra is mentioned in the Vedas, and is invoked along with other devas, like Agni and Surya. The word Indra comes from indriyan, the senses, so one can say that Indra is the god of the body. In Puranic stories, that come 2000 years later, a new word emerges—Bhagavan, God, of the atma, soul. The world of devas is the external world of prakriti and sanskriti, nature and culture. The world of God is internal, psychological, a world of mind and soul. Thus there occurs a shift from the external world of the Vedic tradition to the internal world of the Puranic tradition. Indra, who was important in the Vedic period, became less important in the Puranic period. So while he was invoked in yagnas, no temple was built for him.

Indra is known to be rich, leading an easy, luxurious life. But why does he have to constantly fight with the asuras?

Indra exists not just in Hinduism but also in Buddhism and Jainism. He is the god of luxury and his abode, Indra-loka, is called Swarga or paradise. There's a beautiful garden there called Nandankanan, which is the home of the Kalpataru, the wish-fulfilling tree, a cow called Kamadhenu who grants all wishes, and a jewel called Chintamani which, when held in one's hand, fulfils all desires. Indra has everything; he watches apsaras dance and hears gandharvas sing. Basically, he's having a party all the time.

Asuras are always attacking Indra-loka. It indicates that despite all his riches, all his powers, Indra does not have peace of mind. He's always seeking bhoga—material wealth, pleasure. But it doesn't occur to him that what he has, others don't; what we know today as the *haves* and *have-nots*. So the have-nots are bound to attack him. Devas and asuras are actually half-brothers, both being the sons of Brahma. But the devas are rich and the asuras, poor; one is in Swarga, the other in Patala. It is similar to unrest within a family over the division of wealth. Perhaps these stories were told to awaken the kings of those times to the fact that while they were leading a life of luxury and enjoying themselves in the palace, neighbouring kings or their own subjects might be leading a life of deprivation. In this scenario, tension and struggle are inevitable, and to show this the endless deva–asura sangram, the war between devas and asuras, was created.

In the famous story where Krishna saves the people of Vrindavana from the wrath of Indra, doesn't Indra seem to be misusing his powers against powerless human beings?

This is a story from the Bhagavata Purana, composed 2000 years ago. It was a time when a shift was taking place, and there was tension between the devas and Bhagavan. Today we address both as Bhagavan, but deva and Bhagavan are two different entities, like junior and senior manager. The deva is junior, Bhagavan is senior. Devas are related to all things of the external realm, like Surya, Chandra, stars, indriyan, body, wealth. Bhagavan is associated with the mann, atma, the internal world.

In the story, Krishna tells his people to worship not the gods who are far away but the ones closer to you, inside you. The rain that Indra uses to punish the villagers is uncertain—it may come, it may not. If it's too much or too little, it becomes a cause of suffering. The rains are a symbol for shifting, unreliable emotions. Govardhan Parvat is a symbol for that which is stable, like the atma. So, the internal world gains more importance than the material, external world. Indra slowly becomes an old deva, of bhoga, of partaking in the material world. Through stories, there is a movement towards Krishna, towards bhakti, devotion. It took a long time, nearly 1000 years, for this shift to take place.

There is a story in which Indra asks his most beautiful apsara, Menaka, to disturb the tapasya, deep meditation, of Rishi Vishwamitra. Why is Indra so insecure despite being

the king of devas? He fights with asuras, feels threatened by a rishi ...

A clear division took place when Puranic stories were written 2000 years ago. One kind of stories were about Indra's abode, Swarga, and the other about Vishnu's, Bhagavan's abode, Vaikuntha. Swarga has prosperity but no happiness. Vaikuntha has both. Swarga places more importance on material things, which are all impermanent, so Indra's position is never secure. It is said that by doing 1000 yagnas you can become Indra. So he feels an asura, a raja or even a rishi can, through tapasya, take away his throne. These stories reveal the psychology of insecurity that comes with wealth and success. If you meet highly successful people, you'll be surprised to see they're suspicious, jealous, unhappy—this is the Indra tatva, quality of Indra, in them. Because there is no atma-gyan, self-awareness, therefore, despite his lifestyle of the rich and famous, Indra is not at peace. Whereas Vishnu reclines with ease in Vaikuntha, with Lakshmi by his side; he's contented because he's self-aware. These stories convey that while bhoga is important, and has its own value, you cannot attain happiness through bhoga alone; atma-gyan is as important, and should be pursued simultaneously. That is, you need both Lakshmi, the goddess of wealth, and Saraswati, the goddess of learning.

In names like Narendra, Surendra, what is the meaning of the suffix -indra?

When used as a common noun, the word indra means leader. Surendra means leader of the devas (from sura + indra), Narendra means leader of human beings (nara + indra),

Dharmendra means leader of religion (dharma + indra). So, indra is associated with king, leadership, royalty.

Tell us a story of a battle between Indra and asuras.

All the stories of Indra's battles with asuras are more or less the same. There are different asuras, like Andhaka, Mahisha, Hiranyaksha, Hiranyakashipu, but the story remains the same, much like popular Hindi films! The asura does tapasya, receives a boon from Brahma and launches an attack on Swarga. Since Indra has been leading a cosy life, he doesn't have the strength to fight back, so he loses to the asura. Indra then goes to Brahma who tells him to seek the help of Vishnu, Shiva or Devi. One of them helps him defeat the asura and he is reinstated in Swarga. You may think this is going to end happily, as in fairy tales, but no, the story will be repeated with another asura.

Our stories are always cyclical. There are no full stops, only commas. Indra achieves success, becomes lazy, loses his kingdom, works hard to regain it, becomes lazy again, and it goes on in this fashion. The ritu chakra, circle of seasons, or circle of life, continues.

8

Boons and Curses

In all the stories in the Puranas, the lives of the characters change drastically because of just one shraap, curse, or vardaan, boon. What are these boons and curses, and why are our stories full of them?

We want to know the reason for everything that happens in our lives. This is specific to human beings because they have a mind and can think. Animals don't question what happens to them. All cultures in the world have different explanations. Some say it's because of God, others ascribe it to Shaitan, Satan, and still others to bhoot, ghosts. The Vedas say that everything happens because of us. Every karma, action, is a seed, and every action has a reaction. Thus, when something good happens, people say it is because you did some punya, good deed, in the past, be it a few hours, years or births earlier. Likewise, you must've committed a paap, sin, to be suffering in the present.

Stories were created so that common people could understand this philosophy of karma–punya–paap in the Puranas. To explain punya, vardaan was used, and shraap for paap. If you've done good by someone, he will grant you a boon—implying that you've done punya. If you've hurt someone, he'll curse you, because you've done paap. It is a narrative device. Basically, it's the karma-based philosophy of Hinduism, Jainism and Buddhism, the three main systems that were born in India. In no other culture or religion is karma a central theme. If you read Greek mythology or the Bible, you will not find boons or curses. Even if they are given, they come from a god. In our stories, like the Puranas, the Ramayana and the Mahabharata, even humans can curse each other, not only gods or goddesses. For instance, Urvashi curses Arjuna, Rishi Gautama curses Ahalya, and so on.

There is an interesting story about Rishi Bhrigu. During the battle between asuras and devas, the losing asuras take refuge in Bhrigu's ashram. When the devas try to attack them in Bhrigu's absence, the rishi's wife petrifies their leader, Indra. Later, when Vishnu tries to help the devas, she warns him of dire consequences, upon which Vishnu beheads her. Bhrigu returns to the ashram just then, and witnesses the horrific event. Aggrieved and furious, he curses Vishnu: he will have to take birth on earth and experience death three times.

Commonly in stories, rishis always curse others—why do they do that?

For us the word rishi evokes someone knowledgeable and wise. However, in Puranic stories, rishis have a special role. rishis are tapasvis, those who meditate. Tapasvis save all their energy, or tap (also a word for heat), which accumulates over time as though in a savings account, and it becomes their power.

Gradually, it grows into ojas, spiritual vigour or strength, and then comes siddhaprapti, that is, they achieve siddha—perfection, realization, etc. The power of their siddha is so great that it can change the world. Why does a rishi want that power? Because he wants mukti, moksha—release—from samsaric life, the mortal world. But the world does not leave him alone. It keeps tempting him—positively or negatively. When something makes him happy, he grants a vardaan. By doing this, he ends up taking action; and once a karma is done he is again involved in the mortal world. Likewise, if he gets angry and gives a shraap, he is drawn in again. The message behind these stories is that great power should not be misused, for it can entrap you, prevent you from achieving mukti. Samsara, prakriti, nature, is mayavi—one whose transience is bewitching—and it constantly tries to shackle you to itself by inciting you to act.

Do rishis have so much power that they can curse even the gods?

Nobody is outside the laws of prakriti; its rules apply to everyone. Devas, asuras, gandharvas, yakshas, rakshasas, humans, animals—all kinds of creatures can be cursed. They are all locked within karma, or indrajaal, the web of the senses. For instance, if you do something the other person does not like, he can curse you, or you might receive a boon if they like something you do. Even the gods cannot escape it, be it positive or negative action. Among gods and humans, anyone can grant the other a boon or curse the other. In this respect, there is little difference between them in the Puranic stories. This is a unique feature of our mythology. Brahma, Vishnu, Shiva, all have been cursed.

Who decides what is paap and what is punya?

This is a difficult question. Let me explain it through a story. Krishna is considered a hero, while his mother's brother, Kamsa, is seen as a villain. Krishna goes to Mathura and kills him in a wrestling match. Now, is this good or bad? Normally, killing your relative would be considered bad. But because Krishna has killed a tyrant, people say it's a good deed, punya. In retellings, the story usually stops here, but the Bhagavata Purana takes it further.

Kamsa's father-in-law was Jarasandha, king of Magadha, both of whose daughters were married to Kamsa. Jarasandha, angered by the killing of his son-in-law, attacks Mathura and ultimately burns down the city. Krishna and the Yadava clan have to move to Dwarka as refugees.

So was the killing of Kamsa good or bad? It was good in the short term but not so in the long term. It is never clear-cut whether karma is a paap or a punya. You can never be sure whether Krishna's action was a shraap or a vardaan.

Is it possible that a vardaan is bad and a shraap is good?

You always have to ask when it is good, and whom it is good for. A packet of chips may be good because it's tasty in the short term, but it will make you ill later. You may enjoy it yourself, but when others have to tend to you in ill health, it's not good for them. A situation cannot be judged in isolation—in stories it is told from many different perspectives to see who benefits when.

For instance, Bhishma's father grants him the boon of icchhamrityu, of choosing when to die. Is this good or bad? Bhishma declares he will not die until all the problems of the

Kuru clan are solved. The problems, however, seem to be never-ending. He witnesses the birth of his nephews, then his grand-nephews, and even their children, but he refuses to die. He becomes like a large banyan tree under whose shadow no one else can grow. Because he wishes to take all decisions, resolve all disputes, he prevents succession from taking place. So his boon becomes a curse for others. Finally, Krishna intervenes and has Arjuna pin him down with arrows, because everything must have an 'expiry date'!

Curses and boons usually go to the extremes. Has this ever changed? Is there a middle path?

Everybody says hurtful things when upset. Even if it is followed by an apology, the initial hurt does not disappear. A broken string can only be knotted back together, it can never become whole again. Curses too can be modified later. Take Kumbhakarna's story. Kumbhakarna undergoes tapasya, pleases Brahma who grants him a boon. Kumbhakarna wants to ask for Indra's throne, Indra-asana, but he ends up saying Nidra-asana, a place to sleep. Ravana intervenes to explain that his brother spoke in error, and requests Brahma to change the boon. Brahma modifies it so that Kumbhakarna can wake up for one day every six months. On that day he will be invincible, but if you wake him up at the wrong time, he will die. So what was a vardaan became a curse, and is modified.

In the famous story of Shakuntala, a furious Rishi Durvasa curses her and says that the lover because of whom she neglected her duty towards Durvasa will forget her. When other rishis plead with Durvasa to withdraw the curse, he modifies it—as long as she has his keepsake in her possession, he says, her lover will remember her. But, then, for the drama to unfold a series of events takes place that separate and eventually reunite the lovers. Here the curse becomes a narrative device to move the plot forward.

Although the vardaan of immortality is denied to everyone, it is normally the asuras who are wont to ask for it, because the devas have partaken of Amrita. But they too are not immortal, since during pralaya, doomsday, everything will be wiped out. That nothing is permanent is a running theme.

Since asuras are never granted immortality, they seek the next best option. For instance, Mahisha-asura cunningly asks to be made invincible against devas, asuras, gandharvas, men, but he doesn't mention women. The devas exploit this loophole and Durga is able to kill him. Hiranyakashipu's famous boon is that he cannot be killed above or below, during day or night, at the hands of man or beast, so God takes the form of Narasimha—half-man, half-lion—and kills him balanced on his thigh, on the threshold at twilight.

The concept of the loophole is important; Indians find it very useful. Like when people visit an astrologer and he reads the stars as being unfavourable, they ask him to find a loophole where intervention is possible. So, devas, asuras, humans, and especially Indians, are always on the lookout for a bypass!

Which is the most intelligent curse?

Through the medium of boons and curses, stories can change dramatically. In the Ramayana, you feel sorry for King Dashratha because his favourite son, Rama, is going into vanavas, exile, for fourteen years. But you come to know that Dashratha had once mistakenly killed Shravan Kumar, the only son of a blind couple. They cursed that he would die pining for his son. This tells you that Dashratha is simply suffering due to his past sins, it is his paap ka phal, his just deserts. Suddenly, the perspective shifts—the villain becomes victim, and vice versa. You could say this is an 'intelligent' shraap!

Can I curse my husband?

If a human being can grant a vardaan, he can curse as well. So can you. But there is no certainty whether it will have an effect or not; there is no proof of it.

9

Heaven and Hell

Tell us a bit about Swarga and Naraka.

There is a lot of confusion about heaven and hell as there are different views in different belief systems. India has a variety of faiths—Christianity, Islam, Hinduism, Buddhism, Jainism, and so on—and their concepts have got mixed up, like a khichdi! Traditions like Christianity and Islam believe that you are born once and die once whereas the Vedic tradition believes in rebirth, that is, creatures die and are reborn many times. In cultures with the concept of one life, one death, it is believed that if you follow the rules God has made, you go to Swarga or Jannat (heaven) when you die, and if you break them, you go to Naraka or Jahannam (hell). However, within the concept of rebirth, God has not made any rules. Your karma, actions, in the present life decides where you will end up in your next life, and so on and so forth. Good deeds will lead you to Swarga and bad to Naraka, but the concept here is not like Jannat or Jahannam. It is temporary. Swarga here is not heaven but Indra-loka, the abode of Indra in the skies, and Naraka is not hell but Yama-loka, the abode of Yama underground.

There can be a further complexity in this. For instance, in the Puranas, there is a river called Vaitarni, which an atma, soul, crosses after death to reach Pitr-loka (the land of ancestors). There it stays till it is time for its rebirth. If it is reborn in a good place, the atma can be said to have reached Swarga, otherwise Naraka. Here, Swarga and Naraka become symbols, metaphors.

Who decides whether your karma is good or bad?

In Hinduism, God is not a judge, like in Islam and Christianity where he makes rules for people to follow. Here, different communities and traditions have their own man-made rules. For instance, according to some, if you practise ahimsa, non-violence, you go to Swarga. But in the Ramayana and the Mahabharata there is a lot of violence.

Which leads me to the question: how is it that the Kauravas went to Swarga but the Pandavas didn't?

The Mahabharata's ending is controversial. It tries to explain the complexity of karma, and how difficult it is to decide what is good and what is bad. What happens after the war? The Kauravas lose and the Pandavas win and rule over Hastinapur for thirty-six years, after which they proceed to vanaprastha ashram, the life of the forest, in order to renounce the world. Then they say they'll head to Swarga. They believe they've ruled well, have followed dharma, so they decide to walk to Swarga. Their aspiration is to reach there while still alive. As they climb the mountain, one after the other, the Pandava brothers start dying. Yudhishtira doesn't turn back even once to look at them, or at Draupadi when she dies, because he believes he has renounced everything. He thinks if he is meant to reach Swarga, he will, otherwise he too will die.

He keeps walking and when he reaches the top of the Himalayas, he is greeted by Indra. 'You have been the true Dharmaraj by being virtuous at all times, so come to Swarga,' Indra tells him. Yudhishtira has a dog with him who has followed him from the palace. He requests Indra to allow the dog to enter, but Indra refuses. Yudhishtira says he'll enter only if the dog is allowed, since they have been companions in the long journey, otherwise both will stay out. Indra is very pleased by his principled stand and says, 'You *deserve* to enter heaven.' Yudhishtira enters Swarga to the sound of conch shells and a grand welcome from everyone, including the Kauravas who greet him warmly. Yudhishtira is shocked to see them and asks Indra how the Kauravas came to be in heaven when they were the cause of war, were adharmis. Indra tells him that according to the rules, all those who die at Kurukshetra doing their duty as Kshatriyas, warriors, will find a place in heaven. That is to say, if you follow your caste dharma in the punya bhoomi, holy land, you will achieve Swarga. This is more complicated than simply good or bad karma.

'So where are my brothers?' asks Yudhishtira. Indra takes him to a place far below the Himalayas, under the earth. It is a horrific, stinking place, full of misery. There, his brothers and wife are suffering for their individual paaps, sins—Bhima for overeating, Arjuna for being insecure, Nakula for being a narcissist, Sahadeva for being arrogant about his knowledge, and Draupadi for preferring Arjuna over her other husbands. Yudhishtira feels that compared to the misdeeds of the deceitful Kauravas, these are small faults of his conscientious kin. But Indra explains that since they died on the paavan bhoomi, pure land, of Kurukshetra, following their caste duty, their bad karma was wiped clean and they attained a place in Swarga.

Yudhishtira is extremely angry about the apparent injustice. He stubbornly refuses to go to heaven. At that moment someone—it's not clear who; it could be Indra or Krishna—says to Yudhishtira: 'Hadn't you given up everything? You did not even look back at your brothers when they died. You said you'd renounced everything but obviously you did not let go of your anger. You defeated and killed the Kauravas, punishing them for their misdeeds. You ruled over their kingdom for thirty-six years—wasn't that punishment enough? But you don't seem to have forgiven them and are angry even now. You are carrying your past baggage and are still attached to your negative emotions, so how can you be in heaven?'

Through this twist, it becomes a philosophical story. In the end, it is not about the physical Swarga or Naraka but a state of mind. Swarga is where you find pleasure and plenty, Naraka is where you suffer. But unless you relinquish all your anger, envy, greed, resentment, etc., you cannot achieve heaven. So, Swarga or Naraka is not outside but inside us.

It is said that not everyone goes to the same Swarga or Naraka—do these places also have VIP sections that can be reserved? Please throw some light on this.

The Garuda Purana says there are different Narakas for different crimes where a variety of punishments are meted out—whiplashes, hot oil, and so on. These are more like stories to scare children with. Similarly, there are different Swargas too. Just like in a skyscraper, the 'floor' you end up on depends on your karma—you can reach the higher levels with good karma, or find yourself in the basement through bad. As this philosophy is about rebirth, your levels will keep changing through different births. This is samsara, the eternal cycle of birth and death. Mukti, release, from this can come only when you relinquish your anger, greed, etc.; only when you let go of both attachment and detachment can you leave the building. The Kauravas and Pandavas too will not stay forever in either Swarga or Naraka. The cycle will continue. Nothing is permanent, that's the philosophical underpinning.

Devas and devis live in Swarga, and Shaitan in Naraka. Does that make Yama a Shaitan?

The figure of Shaitan, Satan, comes not from the Puranas but from Islam and Christianity. Since in India everything is mixed up, Hindus too use these words. The Puranas talk about asuras who live in Patala, not Naraka; there's a separate place for them. Yama does not live in Naraka but in Pitr-loka. Yama, the god of accounting, keeps a record of our karma, a balance sheet of sorts. Bear in mind that this is different from being a judge. When you die and cross the Vaitarni to get to Pitr-loka, he opens the account of your karma and calculates your debts. Accordingly, he assigns you a new location or birth—in Swarga or Naraka, as pashu, animal, or pakshi, bird, rich or poor, as Brahmin or Kshatriya or Shudra, male or female, disabled or not, and so on. Chitragupta is his assistant who helps him process all the data. Together they decide into which yoni, womb, you'll be born. After 84 lakh yonis you are granted a human birth, which is a very significant opportunity, because only through the human body can you seek and achieve mukti. If you lose the chance, you'll again have to go through the cycle of 84 lakh lives. So, there's an urgent need to start doing tapasya—it's a long process!

Yama is usually depicted as a funny character whom no one takes seriously. Can you tell us a story about him?

Yama is, in fact, a very tragic character. It is because the subject of death is so grave and depressing that storytellers try to lighten the mood by portraying Yama in a comic way. But the story of Yama is one of the oldest in the Vedas. You may not find other devas or devis there, but Yama is always mentioned.

The story goes that the first humans were the twins—Yama and Yami. Yami says to Yama, 'Although I'm your sister, I'll have to become your wife, otherwise how will we propagate life?' Yama says, 'It won't be right, and I cannot allow this.' Yami agrees. When Yama dies and goes to Pitr-loka, he becomes its first entrant. Since he has no children, he is trapped and cannot be reborn. The word pu-tra comes from 'put' (pron. *putta*)—that Naraka to which you go if you haven't borne children, that is, put-ra, son, or put-ri, daughter. This is why in our culture there are elaborate rituals for childless couples, like in Gaya, Bihar, there's a special shraadh ceremony, and so on.

Yami cries for her brother who she knows will never return. Her tears become the river Yamuna. That is one part of her. The other part becomes ratri, or night. Yamini means night-time. If Yama is daytime, Yamini is night-time, and the two can never meet. It is a story of separation of the first two humans and siblings who can never be together for moral reasons. It may be a metaphor or an allegory, but it's been told since Vedic times. It's not usually retold a lot because it's both awkward and tragic. Yama stays trapped in Pitr-loka and comes to Bhu-loka, the place of the living, only when there is a death. So, death is like his highway.

Why do we feed crows to pacify our ancestors during a shraadh ceremony?

This is not appeasement. The belief is that an atma crosses the Vaitarni to Pitr-loka and waits there till its rebirth. The children it has left behind on earth are duty-bound to beget children so that it can be reborn and return. Till that time, the ancestor doesn't get food in Pitr-loka. During Pitr Pakshya, that is, shraadh, a pind daan is done for ancestors, where rice balls, pind are offered, daan. The three pinds represent three parts of a person—mind, body and soul or, some say, mind and body and karma. The grain is crushed before being given because dead ancestors don't have teeth. The belief is that Yama's messengers come in the form of crows.

We know that crows say 'Ka, ka, ka', which is an important letter in the Vedas. Our alphabet too starts with ka. All questions—kyun (why), kab (when), kaise (how)—begin with ka. So the crows' cawing is like your ancestors asking you, 'Kya?'—'What are you doing with your life?' In the event of death, you are reminded about your life and its purpose. Here, the offering of grain, anna, is very significant. You are made of anna—in Sanskrit the word for flesh, or body, is annakosh. You are alive because of anna, but what are you doing with it? This entire ritual of Pitr Pakshya has been devised for you to remember your ancestors and to reflect on your own life.

10

Shakti

What is shakti? Is it the concept of divine cosmic energy? Is it a devi?

The Puranas use literary devices like metaphors, idioms, stories to convey concepts. There are two parallel forces in the universe. One is the inanimate, material force, which is tangible, sagun. The other is the one with life, prana shakti, which is intangible, nirgun. Trees, colours and even gender, among other things, can be used as a means of expressing a thought. So, the sagun has been described through the female form and the nirgun through the male form. Our human body is split into two parts: the perceptible, palpable flesh, sagun, and the mind, which cannot be seen or touched, nirgun. The former is called prakriti, nature, shakti, and the latter is atma, soul. Once the atma leaves the body, the body becomes lifeless, although you can still see and feel it. prakriti remains, and that is the feminine aspect. In Sanskrit, it is called the world of naam and roop, that is, name and appearance, which is identifiable, thus sagun; the other world is different from or beyond this.

There are fascinating stories about devis like Saraswati, Parvati and Lakshmi, in which they invariably have a more significant role to play than the male gods. Please throw some light on this.

If you look at it from a feminist angle, it's a male–female divide, but if you look at it spiritually, the male gods—the Trimurti (Brahma, Vishnu and Shiva)—are creating, sustaining and destroying. All these are action words, verbs. On the other hand, Saraswati is associated with knowledge, Lakshmi with wealth, Durga with shakti, power—all these are nouns. Knowledge, wealth and power exist in the world, but you need someone to create, sustain and destroy them. Similarly, in grammar, you need both verb and noun to form a sentence. Male forms are associated with verbs and female forms with nouns, and together they form language.

The three devis are forms of Shakti and are the consorts of the three gods. Aren't the Tridevi superior to the Trimurti?

You cannot separate devas and devis. Different sects have different beliefs: in the Shakta tradition, the Goddess is most superior, whereas in the Vaishnava tradition it is Vishnu. But taken together there is no clear case for one being superior to the other. Just like man and woman, one cannot exist without the other. This is represented in Shiva's Ardhanareshwara form, where he is half-man, half-woman. In many temples, you will find depictions of dampatya, married couple, to show this principle. To live, you need both mind and body; you cannot separate them.

There is a saying that Shiva without Shakti is shav, dead. Tell us about this.

There is a story about a time when, upset by Shiva's aloofness towards her, Parvati leaves him, saying he doesn't realize that he needs her for it is she who looks after him and his devotees. Later, Shiva witnesses a famine and people leaving for Kashi because it is fertile. He finds Parvati feeding people and asks her for food, saying he needs her.

The philosophy here is that the living will always experience hunger because they have a body to sustain. This is a story about hunger. Shiva is a great tapasvi and a god, and has conquered hunger. Devi tells him, 'You may be great but not your devotees who still feel hungry. Will you tell them to meditate or give them food?' The story talks of the basic reality of life.

Sometime during the ancient period, sages began giving sermons about relinquishing desire to obtain moksha, and so on. Women said that while these ideas were profound, children would still bawl with hunger. The husbands wished to settle in dhams, holy places, and become vairagis. But even they would feel hungry towards the evening. The women told their menfolk that unless they worked, tilled the fields, engaged in trade, etc., they could not expect to run the household. This concept is illustrated through the simple exchange between Shiva and Shakti.

The form of Shakti here is Annapurna, who tells Shiva that on Kailasa, where he resides, no one is hungry, but in Kashi, where ordinary people reside, everyone feels hungry. Will Shiva not serve them? So, Shiva descends from Kailasa to Kashi, and becomes Shankara Bhagavan who grants people vardaan and food. It is interesting that Annapurna, the goddess of the kitchen, who cooks food, is married to Shiva who is never in need of food—so, whom is she cooking for? And Shiva is known as bhiksha-tan, he who asks for alms of food; since he never feels hungry, he is asking not for himself but for his devotees.

The dual message here is that while you seek food, you should also prevent your hunger from growing out of proportion, otherwise it gives rise to greed. There's also a concept of striking a balance between greed and contentment. Shiva is talking of contentment, while Shakti is focused on food and other desires. We have to find equilibrium between becoming greedy and renouncing the world.

There is a famous story about Devi Mahatmya. During festivals in south India, plays based on this story are performed. Tell us about this form of the Devi.

Devi Mahatmya is a famous story about Durga. Durga is worshipped in Bengal during Dussehra, in Gujarat during Navaratri when the garba dance happens, during the jagrata in north India, etc. Devi Mahatmya came in late after Vishnu Purana but is very powerful, and probably arose out of folklore.

The story goes that the asura king Rambha and Princess Mahishi get married and have a son, Mahisha-asura, who can take the form of an animal at will. After years of doing penance, he is granted a boon by Brahma: no deva, asura, animal, or even the Tridev can kill him. Mahisha gains immense power and defeats all the devas of Indra-loka easily. A troubled Indra seeks the help of the Trimurti. They find a loophole in the boon, and create a woman. Shiva gives her his trishul, Indra gives her his vajra, Agni gives her a bhal and Surya gives her the power of ten thousand suns. Raja Himavan gives her a lion as a vehicle and Vishnu gives her the name Durga. With this arsenal, Durga fights a pitched battle, and the number of dead asuras, rakshasas and elephants keeps rising. The last asura to enter the battlefield is Mahisha and the battle intensifies. Mahisha keeps changing forms to attack her, but she destroys each one, ultimately killing him with Shiva's trishul.

If you observe the idol of Durga carefully, she is dressed in red, in jewels, and looks like a bride, but she has weapons in her hands and is killing a buffalo. It is a violent image. The concept here is that for bhoga, to satiate hunger, you need to offer sacrifice, to kill. Even for cultivation, you burn a forest, kill snakes, rats. So whether it is vegetarian or non-vegetarian, food is acquired through violence. Grihastha jeevan, the householder's life—where there is dhan, dhanya, sampatti, wealth—entails violence. The extent of violence depends on your viveka, conscience. This is the niyam, rule, of prakriti.

Devi has taken the extreme forms of Parvati and Durga. How so?

It's like us human beings. We have different personae in different situations, as with children, parents, our superiors, when we serve, and so on. Devis and devas too change according to the circumstances. These stories are very intimate, drawn from human life and issues. For instance, when we get angry we take on the form of Rudra, but at other moments, we can take on the calm aspect of Shiva as well.

Did the Devi come before Bhagavan or after?

This is a very political question; if women are seeing this, I have to say the Devi came first! Anyhow, this is a spiritual, philosophical, metaphysical subject. No one can say who came first, the man or the woman. We're all equal, and the order of appearance doesn't suggest that one is greater than the other.

In the Shakta tradition, Devi came first; in the Vaishnava tradition, Vishnu came first. Natural historians would say that prakriti existed before human beings and will continue to exist after them. If we see prakriti in the female form, Devi is eternal. Prakriti is the canvas on which a painting is made; the act of painting is masculine as it's a verb. In the Puranas, Shakti is both mother and daughter. The mother is Prakriti, nature, and the daughter is Sanskriti, culture.

This is a metaphor, only meant to indicate a deeper concept. When taken literally, it loses its bhaav, essence. Everyone has a role in the Brahmanda, the universe, which comprises male and female, Shiva and Shakti.

11

Ganesha

In the Puranas, the most famous god, with four arms and an elephant head, is Ganesha. What is the reason for his popularity?

Ganesha is a mysterious god; no scholar can say for sure when and why Ganesha became popular. The words ganapati and ganesha are found in the Vedas, but we don't know whether these refer to the same Gajanana, the elephant-headed god whom we worship today. Gana means gang, tribe, group of people; Ganapati means leader of the people. The Indus Valley civilization, which pre-dates Vedic times, had elephant seals. Clearly, people knew about elephants. But the idols and images of Ganesha began to emerge only 1500 years ago whereas the Vedas go back 4000 years. So this is a development of the late Puranic times.

Ganesha acquired huge importance around this time. Adi Shankaracharya, writing 1000 years ago, says that like the Shaiva, Vaishnava and Shakta traditions, there was also a Ganpatya tradition. In this tradition, devotees worshipped Ganesha, they knew God through Ganesha.

There is a clearer reason for his popularity in recent times. In Maharashtra, in the seventeenth and eighteenth centuries, the Peshwas came to power after King Shivaji Maharaj. These leaders of the Maratha community—Gaekwad, Holkar, and so on—worshipped Ganesha as their ishta-devata, personal deity. Wherever they went, they took the Ganesha puja with them. Until then, among Brahmins ganesha had been only a word in mantras, but because of the Maratha confederacy, stories and images of Ganesha started becoming very popular.

So, Ganesha was merely mentioned in the texts from the Vedic up to the early Puranic period. It was in the late Puranic times that he gained importance, which was further established by the Peshwas. And later, of course, there was Bollywood!

It is said that Ganesha is the son of Shiva and Shakti, but there is confusion as to whether he is Shiva's or Parvati's son.

Ganesha is called ayonija, someone who's not born from a womb. Shakti asks Shiva for a child, but he says he's not interested since he is eternal, anant, and goes away. She decides to have a baby without him—bina nayak, without man, that is, Vinayaka. She rubs haldi, turmeric, on her body, and then sculpts a beautiful doll from its scrapings, does pran-pratishtha on it and breathes life into it. Thus Vinayaka is born. She asks Vinayaka to guard the entrance of her cave. Shiva arrives and asks for his wife, Shakti, wondering who the child is. Vinayaka, following instructions, does not let him pass. A battle ensues between them, and since Shiva is so powerful, he cuts off Vinayaka's head with his trishul. Upon seeing this, Shakti begins to weep. When Shiva asks her where the child came from, she tells him that she doesn't need him to produce a child, she can have one on her own. This indicates the power of prakriti, who does not need gods to create life. Shakti becomes livid and takes on a terrifying form. To appease her, Shiva says he will bring Vinayaka back to life, but for that he needs another head. He sends his ganas, followers, telling them to bring the head of the first creature they see facing north. The people spot an elephant. They bring his head and Shiva does pran-pratishtha and brings the child back to life. This child has got his body from his mother and head from his father, and is thus born of both.

The story is interesting because it unites the Shaiva and Shakta traditions. Because of Ganesha, the ugra, terrifying, Kali becomes the maternal, domestic Gauri, and the sanyasi Shiva becomes a father and a grihastha, householder. This transformation is an important concept in Hinduism. Ganesha thus becomes the god of grihastha jeevan, domestic life.

In the Vedas, Ganapati was merely a leader of people; in the Puranas, Shiva declares him the leader of Shiva's followers, saying that Ganesha will be worshipped before everyone. It is people's belief that these two Ganapatis are the same, but we can't be sure.

Let's talk a little about the symbols of Ganesha. He has an elephant head and his vahana, vehicle, is a tiny rat. How are his symbols so unique?

Ganesha functions as a uniter of different thoughts. He is associated with both the goddess of wealth, Lakshmi, and the goddess of learning, Saraswati. The elephant itself is a symbol of wealth and power, Lakshmi, but is said to have a strong memory and great knowledge, Saraswati. Riddhi and Siddhi, his wives, are associated with wealth and learning respectively. His rotund belly is linked with that of a trader's, who keeps counting his money (wealth), as well as of a Brahmin's as he leads a sedentary life (knowledge). In one of his hands, he carries Ankush, a goad, which is used to push and pull a large animal like an elephant. In another hand, he carries Parashu, an axe, the symbol of analysis, of breaking down a problem into smaller parts. In yet another hand, he carries a paash, string, which is a symbol of synthesis, joining. Thus Ganesha both breaks down and unites—these are the intellectual concepts. His vehicle is a rat. In India, where agriculture is the largest occupation, the rat is the biggest enemy of the farmer community. It represents problems, and Ganesha holds down the problem, keeps it under control. A naga, snake, winds itself around his belly like a belt. Snakes prey upon rats. But here, both predator and prey reside contentedly with Ganesha; the snake will not attack the rat and the rat will not steal grain from the fields.

All these ideas are embodied in Ganesha. In a film, when there are many ideas driving a scene, and a lot is happening at the level of symbols—in the background and the foreground—it has an immense effect. Similarly for a work of art—it stimulates thought. Among all the gods and goddesses in Hinduism, Ganesha is associated with the maximum number of symbols. Due to this, he has many roops, forms, and devotees can represent him as they wish, in the form of Vishnu or Shiva—these days he is even seen taking a selfie! This amorphous quality of Ganesha is very important; this is what has made him so popular. Nowadays, even his potbelly has been replaced with six-pack abs, although that's not ideal because the potbelly invites wealth!

Ganesha is known as Vighna-karta and Vighna-harta—both a creator and remover of obstructions. How is that?

Ganesha gained importance in the Puranic period. Before that, perhaps people were scared of elephants, especially wild elephants. In open fields, a wild elephant is extremely dangerous whereas a domestic one, considered cuddly and cute, is a useful animal. The domestic elephant is also a symbol of royalty, as it was kept by kings. An elephant, thus, evokes paradoxical feelings—of fear as well as love. This bhava, emotion, is associated with the idol of Ganesha.

We can speculate that earlier, he was a feared gramadevata, village deity, whom people prayed to in order to keep elephants away. Gradually, when he came to be associated with Shiva, Shakti, Lakshmi, Saraswati, he became the god of good luck and auspiciousness, a beloved god who removes obstructions, vighna, and is welcomed into homes. Now we do Ganesha puja so that there is prosperity, affluence and well-being everywhere.

There is a famous story about the king of wealthy Lanka, Kubera, being taught a lesson in humility by Ganesha. What is the meaning of that story?

In the story, when Kubera feeds Ganesha in order to display his wealth, Ganesha's hunger is not satiated even after he polishes off all the food in Kubera's kingdom. Distraught and apologetic, Kubera goes to Shiva for advice, and Shiva tells him that like Kubera's greed for wealth, Ganesha's hunger too cannot be satisfied unless he is offered food with devotion. An enlightened Kubera goes back and serves Ganesha a little bit of leftover rice and Ganesha is immediately sated.

If you observe the symbolism, both Kubera and Ganesha are rotund, and are associated with being fat. They are both yakshamurtis, as is the laughing Buddha. Traditionally, a yakshamurti is associated with wealth, prosperity and contentment. One is physical comfort and the other is mental. These are two different emotions; one does not necessarily lead to the other. What it indicates is that merely bhoga, partaking of material riches, does not satisfy. The difference between animals and humans is that animals stop eating as soon as their stomach is full. But a human being is capable of thinking of the hunger of tomorrow, the day after, ten lives ahead, and so on—our hunger can be never-ending. Like Ganesha in the story, we tend to take all that is given, and be endlessly greedy. It is through Ganesha that we understand that although Shiva doesn't have food or wealth, which is what one gets from Kubera, he has the secret of satiation. This is why Shiva is called Kamantaka, one who allays hunger and desire.

We worship Ganesha before starting any new venture which signifies that he's an important god. But Shiva and Vishnu take precedence over him. Why?

Hinduism does not come from one source. There are several streams winding through and intersecting with each other too. One upholds the Trinity—Brahma, Vishnu, Shiva. Another follows the Ganpatya tradition, of Ganapati. Yet another describes Ganesha as uniting the Shaiva and Shakta traditions.

It is also not completely accurate to say that we worship Ganesha before every puja or new venture. In the Shiva Purana or Shiva kathas, it is said that Shiva had granted Ganesha a boon that he would be worshipped before the start of any new venture. But the Shaivas do this, not the followers of Vishnu. The Vaishnavas worship Vishwaksena, who is the leader of their people.

There are different rules everywhere, although nowadays we want to homogenize everything, fix the rules and the place of our gods. It doesn't work like that, because times change and things evolve. Ganapati's own history, his changing roles, indicates how Indian society has changed over time. For instance, in South East Asia, Ganesha is not considered auspicious. His idol is represented with skulls because he's a god of Tantra, who travelled a thousand years from India to South East Asia. This is a terrifying form. There's an image of Shiva as Gajantaka—one who kills an elephant, Gaja-asura and dances with its skin. Now we cannot say whether there is any link between Gaja-asura and Ganapati, but there may be a story there. Another image shows Ganesha in Shiva's lap. Maybe once there was a rivalry, which later matured into tolerance. The negative relationship became a positive one.

We come to understand the psychology of Indian people through such stories. We also see how Hindu religion is so different from others, for it shifts organically. In Mumbai, Ganapati has taken on a new form which didn't even exist 100 years ago—where did this come from?

All these are part of the svayambhu tradition, arising from the devotees' desires. As their experiences and desires changed, so did the traditions, images, stories, ideas. So, Ganesha, today, has become even more popular than the Trimurti.

12

Weapons

It is said that we should follow the path of ahimsa, non-violence. But our devis and devatas are always ready for war, armed with astras, weapons. Why this contradiction?

When the idols of gods and goddesses were made thousands of years ago, astras had a different meaning from the one today, when we associate them with violence. Primitive man was surrounded by plants, trees, animals. For him, his weapon was a means for survival, for hunting and gathering food. Seen in that light, astras are actually instruments or tools, we need them to survive. To cut down trees, to create farms, plough the fields, and so on, you need an astra. Even to cook, you need astras: to chop, to pound, to grind. Boiling, roasting, burning—all these are rather violent activities! Tools are the primary technology for living.

We gradually moved from a primitive to an agrarian society; we grew crops, built houses, amassed grain and wealth. To safeguard our food from theft, we built granaries and fortresses, and began carrying weapons for our own protection. Weapons and tools are important in any culture.

That's why all gods and goddesses have some weapon or the other. Shiva has the trishul, trident, Hanuman has the gada, mace, and Vishnu has various weapons.

Where did Shiva get his trishul from, who made it, and how did it become so integral to his image?

This is a mystery, because nobody made the trishul. Shiva is svayambhu, self-created, born of his own volition, so he was born with the trishul—it's always been there. It is a metaphor. Shiva is always associated with three things—three eyes, three leaves of the bel plant, and the three lines of bhabhuti or ash smeared on his forehead—so his weapon has to be a special spear with three blades, the trishul. It is said that this indicates Tri-loka, the three worlds—Swarga-loka, Bhu-loka and Patala. In the Bhagavad Gita it is associated with the three gunas, or qualities—rajasguna (royal, rich), tamasguna (dark, heavy), satvaguna (pure, light).

In Puranic stories, Shiva uses his trishul just once, to kill Andhaka-asura who has the same qualities as another asura, Raktabeej. Every drop of his blood that is spilt creates another Andhaka. Shiva impales him with his trishul till all the blood is drained from his body. Andhaka prays to Shiva and becomes a rishi who doesn't have a single drop of blood remaining in his body. All the bad blood has been drained out of him. The contact with the trishul converts him into Shiva's bhakt, devotee.

In fact, Shiva, and most other gods and goddesses for that matter, are usually associated with the bow. One can see it literally or as a metaphor. The bow is related to Yoga-shastra, the teachings about yoga, a form of physical and mental discipline. If you observe a bow, you will notice that it has to be strung very carefully—as is mentioned in the Ramayana as well. If it's too tight, the bow will break; if it's too loose, the bow is useless. The bow is thus a symbol for the mind, which should be balanced; only with a correctly wound bow can you shoot a target. So it becomes a symbol of dhyana, focus, or dharana, awareness. These principles of yoga are explained using the example of a bow, which is perhaps why it is so popular.

One of Shiva's names is Pinaki, where Pinak is the name of his bow. There is an interesting story related to this. Because it's Shiva, everything has to be larger than life! Here, the shaft of Shiva's bow is believed to be Mount Meru and the bowstring is Shesh Naga, king of serpents. The bow shaft symbolizes the axis of space, of the entire universe, and the snake, the bowstring, is associated with time, because it always moves forward—past to present to future—and sheds its skin like changing times. Thus Shiva holds both space and time in his hand.

There are three asuras, Vidyunmali, Tarakaksha and Viryavana, together known as Tripura-asura. They can be killed with an arrow only when aligned one behind the other. Shiva kills Tripura-asura with his magical bow, the Pinak, thus destroying the asuras' three worlds. His arrow is Vishnu himself; his rath, chariot, is Bhu-loka, its wheels the sun and moon, the four books of the Vedas his horses, and Brahma his sarathi, charioteer. But after killing the asuras he feels so remorseful that he smears their ashes on his forehead in three lines. It is a dramatic story, with a fantastical chariot and bow, but there's no trishul here!

Although Vishnu was Shiva's arrow in this story, he himself has so many weapons. Why is that?

It is believed that Brahma is the creator, Shiva the destroyer and Vishnu the protector of the universe. For his role as the sustainer, who manages and preserves society, Vishnu requires many weapons. All his weapons have names—the Sudarshan chakra, a furiously revolving disc on his index finger, which like a boomerang attacks and returns to him. He has a mace in his hand called Kaumodaki, a sword called Nandaka, a bow called Saranga. One of Vishnu's names is Sarangapani, one who holds the Saranga bow. Vishnu's various avatars have different astras. Parashuram has an axe or Parashu. Rama has the familiar bow and arrow; he's also known as Eka-bani, the one with a single baan, arrow, that is, focus. Besides the Sudarshan chakra, Krishna holds all the other weapons as well, because he's the purnavatar, one who's a full avatar of Vishnu. The Kalki avatar has the Nandaka sword. These are all the different stories.

All gods and goddesses have a special connection with their astra. Tell us about Indra's weapon, the Vajra or thunderbolt.

The story goes that an asura by the name of Vrita captures Indra's kingdom. Vrita has a boon that he cannot be defeated by any weapon made of wood or metal. Indra approaches Vishnu for help, who takes him to a meditating rishi, Dadhichi. The rishi has been meditating for many years and has collected a lot of power within himself. At Vishnu's behest, he abandons his body, and the Vajra is made from his bones, more powerful than any existing weapon, which will eventually destroy Vrita.

This is probably a story from the time when weapons and tools were made from bones. Maybe it refers to Ayurveda which claims that siddhi purushas, sages who've accumulated a lot of power, have special bodies—their muscles, sinews, bones, are all very powerful. Their bones are supposed to be stronger than iron. Gaya in Bihar is named after Gaya-asura, who through his meditation had developed such a powerful body that different weapons were created from his bones and muscles, which the gods and goddesses then carried. At some level, all these stories correlate yoga, Ayurveda, tap (meditation) and astra.

This story also illustrates vairagya bhava, the spirit of self-sacrifice. The gods ask for Dadhichi's bones and he willingly gives them away. So a rishi should be detached to such a degree that he can donate his bones. In fact, he is so generous that a king receives his daan. Thus, the Vajra was a daan to Indra.

Did these weapons have a manufacturing unit? Who made them?

Vishwakarma, the devata of craftsmen, made all the weapons. He made the Sudarshan chakra from an ansh, a speck, of Surya, the sun. Different Puranas mention different sources of weapons. In the Mahabharata, when Khandavaprastha is burnt to the ground, the fire god Agni is so happy that he gives the Pandavas all their weapons. Arjun's famous bow, the Gandiva, comes from Agni. In another story, Arjun appeals to Shiva for the Pashupatastra.

Why are the bow and arrow so popular with all the gods and goddesses?

This was probably a new invention at that time. With a stone, a spear or a sword, you could reach only ten or twenty feet ahead, but the bow and arrow made it possible to reach a faraway target. People perhaps felt the gods and goddesses were behind it. It must have had a life-changing impact, like the mobile phone in our times.

But it was more of a metaphor, like the famous bow of Kama, the god of desire. Its shaft is made of sugar cane and the bowstring is made of butterflies and bees, while the arrows are made of flowers. Even he has an apparently 'violent' persona with his weaponry. Shiva, Rama, Vishnu, Devi—all have bows and arrows.

Brahma made the Brahmastra, which is deemed to be ancient India's nuclear weapon. Was it really so powerful?

We actually cannot say what it was. The Puranas were written thousands of years ago and they claimed that the force of devis and devatas could be infused in weapons through mantras, which were considered powerful and extremely valuable. For instance, Rama infused his weapons with the power of agni (fire), vayu (wind) and jal (water). In his war with Ravana he used different kinds of weapons. Some could infuse their weapons with the power of different gods as well, like the Brahmastra, Narayanastra, Vaishnavastra, Shaivastra, Pashupatastra, and so on. There is a detailed description of these, particularly in the Mahabharata.

At the end of the war in the Mahabharata, Ashwatthama, Dronacharya's son, is the only warrior from the Kaurava side left on the battlefield. He invokes the Brahmastra in order to kill the last Pandava heir in Uttara's womb. Uttara is Abhimanyu's wife. Arjun decides to counter it with his own Brahmastra. In all the stories until now, only one Brahmastra has been used at a time, like the one Rama unleashed to kill Ravana. If two Brahmastras were allowed to collide with each other, the impact would be tremendous. The trees would perish, the snow-capped mountains would melt, volcanoes would erupt everywhere—it would be so horrible that the earth itself would be destroyed. Vyasa appears then, and tells them to withdraw their weapons. Warriors in those days had so much power that they could recall even the arrows that had been shot. Arjun withdraws his Brahmastra but Ashwatthama does not have the power to do so. This shows that he is not responsible; he cannot recall his own weapon. Krishna intervenes and stops it, but he curses Ashwatthama that he will never die, and his wounds will fester and become infected and his body will rot forever with unhealed wounds. It is said that he is still alive.

Ashwatthama was cursed for not using weapons responsibly. That is the message here; not whether we had a nuclear weapon but if we were responsible.

13

Sacred Animals

In temples we see idols of animals and birds beside the idols of gods and goddesses. Are all these creatures their vahanas?

In ancient times, different people worshipped different entities—trees, animals, birds, water. As civilization evolved and people started living in communities, forming villages and temples, all these congregated, along with gods, in one temple. Each god came to be associated with one or the other creature, which are known as vahanas in stories. Vahana means that on which you travel, that is, vehicle; in fact, the word wagon comes from vahana.

Do all gods and goddesses have vahanas?

Yes, perhaps because they live to travel but not on foot. Krishna has a bird, Garuda; Varuna has a crocodile for water; Indra has Airavata the elephant; Durga has a wild animal, a tiger; Ishan has a domestic animal, a white bull, and so on.

Is the naga around Shiva's neck his vahana?

No, the naga, or serpent, is a symbol associated with him, as it is with many other gods. Shiva's vahana is Nandi the bull. You'll see an idol of Nandi outside every Shiva temple, as well as a turtle, although the turtle is not his vahana. He travels from Kashi to Kailasa, or anywhere else, riding on Nandi. He's called Vrushabhnath; vrushabh meaning bull, and nath is master, or lord, thus lord of the bull.

A vahana is not only a vehicle; it also indicates its god's temperament. For instance, Shiva is an independent god. He is a tapasvi, a vairagi, whom you cannot domesticate completely. You can domesticate a bull only if you castrate it. Thereafter it is hitched to a bullock cart or a plough, but it cannot be mated with a cow. Only a wild bull can be used for that, though not for ploughing. So it is a wild bull that is associated with Shiva.

If the turtle is not Shiva's vahana, whose vahana is it?

There is always a turtle in front of the Nandi in temples. It is a symbol of yoga; just as a turtle can draw all its legs into its shell, so can a yogi rein in or control his senses. But the turtle is also a vahana—of the river goddess Yamuna. A makar—half-fish, half-elephant—is the vehicle of the goddess Ganga.

What is Brahma's vahana?

Brahma's vahana is the hans, or goose. It is different from a rajhans, swan, although that's what our calendar art depicts. The hans is an important figure in our mythology. A hans looks calm as it swims on the surface although its legs are working very hard under the water. It doesn't allow even a drop of water to touch its feathers. Similarly, a tapasvi too maintains a calm bearing although his mind is working hard, it is turbulent. Nothing attracts or bothers him—success or failure, happiness or sorrow—he keeps his composure through everything. So the word hans is associated with rishis and yogis, and perhaps that's why with Brahma, although in stories he is constantly agitated. The other gods probably asked Brahma to keep the hans so he could learn from it!

Vishnu's vehicle is Garuda, but when he's resting, it's always on Shesh Naga, king of serpents. Garuda is thought to be part eagle, but most likely he is a hawk. In the Vedic period, 4000 years ago, there used to be many complicated rituals, ceremonies but few stories. One of these—agnichayan—used to be performed in a mandap constructed in the shape of a bird. It was done to ask Agni, the fire god, to go up to Swarga and get Amrita from there. This idea of a bird travelling up to heaven and returning with Amrita came from the Vedic period and was gradually converted into a story in the Puranas.

The story is that Rishi Kashyapa had two wives, Kadru and Vinata. Kadru bore the nagas and Vinata gave birth to Garuda. The two sisters were always quarrelling with each other due to sibling rivalry. One day, they wagered about a horse named Ucchaishrava. Kadru said it wasn't all white, and had a black tail. Vinata said it was all white. They bet that whoever lost would become the other's dasi, maidservant. Kadru tells her black naga children to go and attach themselves to the horse's tail so that it appears black from a distance. Thus she wins the bet by deceit, and Vinata becomes her dasi. When she seeks release from this enslavement, Kadru tells her that she will free her only if Vinata brings Amrita for her children. Vinata asks her son Garuda to bring the Amrita. Garuda goes to Swarga, battles with Indra, and fetches the Amrita for the nagas. He knows that the nagas will become all-powerful if he gives them the Amrita, so he tells them to bathe and come, after which he'll serve it to them. While the nagas go for a bath, he returns the Amrita to Indra. Upon their return, when the nagas ask about the Amrita, Garuda says Indra took it away. They ask why he gave it away, and he replies that they never told him not to. They only asked him to bring it. But since he kept his part of the bargain the nagas don't have any choice but to free his mother.

Vishnu, who is watching all this, asks Garuda why he didn't taste the Amrita after taking such pains to bring it from heaven, balanced on his beak. Garuda says he has no desire for it, and that he only wanted to release his mother from bondage. Vishnu says, 'You have an innate power—you don't get entangled in moha and maya, desire and attachment. You are a born tapasvi; will you stay with me?' Garuda puts forward the condition that he'll carry Vishnu and remain below him, but Vishnu will also have to keep Garuda above him. Vishnu wonders how he can manage that, and then puts a flag overhead on his chariot with the symbol of Garuda on it.

The vahana of Saraswati ...

Is also a hans, like Brahma's. If you observe miniature paintings carefully, you'll see her vehicle is depicted as a bagula, crane, which is a symbol of concentration. Different concepts emerge from the different animals.

It's clear that Vaishno Devi's vahana is a lion, but which of the two is Durga's vahana—tiger or lion?

Durga is shown with a lion in Bengal and with a tiger in Punjab, where she is known as Sherawali, but they are understood to be the same goddess. There's a lot of confusion between lions and tigers in India; while African lions are huge, the lions in Gir forests are not as dramatic—they're just like big cats. Asiatic lions were never so powerful, but all over the world lions are a symbol of royalty. Even in places where there have never been any lions, like in China, they are the emblem of the king. The word Singapore means city (pore) of the lion (singha) and Sri Lanka's flag has a lion symbol on it. So, Durga is a goddess of kings. The throne of a king is known as singha-asana—the seat (asana) of a lion (singha).

On the other hand, the tiger is respected all across India. It is known as vyaghra in Sanskrit. A tiger is known to be very protective of its family, and it's beautiful to observe cats in general taking care of their young ones. So, goddesses are usually associated with the cat species, and whether it's a lion or a tiger varies in different states.

You spoke of the cat family. Are dogs too associated with anyone?

Shiva has two roops, one shaant, peaceful, one ugra, ferocious, angry. The former is associated with Nandi the bull, while Bhairava, his ugra roop, is always seen with dogs. Temples with the idol of Mahakaleshwar usually keep a barking dog inside.

Is the owl, often seen in images of Lakshmi, her vahana?

Lakshmi with an owl is seen mostly in Bengal, Odisha, and other eastern regions. But this is not very clear. Some say the owl is a symbol of Alakshmi, Lakshmi's sister, who is associated with violence and fighting. Another theory is that owls eat rats that cause destruction of crops, and thus of wealth—and Lakshmi is the goddess of wealth. Lakshmi is never actually seen riding an owl, so it is not her vehicle. Lakshmi is commonly known as Gajavahini, and seen riding an elephant, gaja, or even with a pair of white elephants who are bathing her with milk with their upraised trunks. So her vehicle may be the elephant. Some people believe that Lakshmi on an owl brings bad luck, but good luck when on an elephant.

Poets used the elephant as a metaphor for clouds, and gajavahana, elephant-vehicle, was very important as it was the vehicle of kings. Indra himself, his Vajra in hand, travels on Airavata, a special elephant with six tusks, seven trunks, and so on. Surya has a seven-horsed chariot, Chandra has an antelope-driven chariot—somewhat like Santa Claus! The figure of Kama is very exciting. He sits on a parrot, tota, and his wife, Rati, on a mynah. The tota–mynah are a famous couple in folklore, and they are actually Kama (lust and romance) and Rati (erotica). These two are deities of the Kama-shastra, treatises on pleasure.

It is said that the creatures associated with gods and goddesses are actually asuras. Is it so?

It has been said in some stories. For instance, in Tamil Nadu, the story of Murugan is quite famous. Murugan is a form of Kartikeya, Shiva's son. He kills Taraka-asura, after which the asura's younger brother Surapadmana attacks him. Before dying, he asks for Murugan's forgiveness. Murugan forgives him and asks him to take the form of a peacock and become his vehicle. So, in this story the peacock is an asura.

In other stories, in south India, Kartikeya sits on a lion because he is associated with Mangal rashi, that is, Mars, which is associated with war. Kartikeya is the commander of war and sometimes has a lion with him, which was supposedly an asura whom he had defeated.

Ganesha's rat is also considered an asura which Ganesha is controlling, so that it does not destroy crops and harm farmers. In other stories, particularly in Maharashtra, Ganesha is also associated with a peacock—thus the phrase 'Ganapati bappa morya' or Moreshwara, the god (ishwar) of the peacock (mor). The peacock is very famous in India, and since it's a beautiful bird all gods and goddesses wish to be associated with it. In paintings, you'll see it with Saraswati; Gauri is offered a peacock feather during Gauri puja, and so on. Krishna sports a peacock feather in his crown, and is, in fact, considered a peacock himself. The gopikas, milkmaids, in his raas-leela are the mornis (peahens). The peacock has become so popular because it is considered a symbol of masculinity.

Krishna is usually seen among cows, but is the cow not his vehicle?

No, a vehicle is always male, never female. A sacrificial animal too is always male. Even the sher is a tiger not a tigress. The buffalo is Yama's vehicle, not Krishna's. It is slow and persistent, like death. From the moment you are born, Yama begins his journey towards you, moving in a straight line like the buffalo, and will surely reach you one day!

What is Rama's vahana?

Vishnu's vehicle is Garuda, but his avatars do not have vehicles. Krishna does not have a vahana, but in stories he is often seen on Garuda. When the Krishna parampara flourished, it was believed that there is no difference between the two, that he is Vishnu himself. In fact, when Indra asks Krishna for protection from an asura, Garuda comes to carry Krishna.

Interestingly, the Garuda that Krishna sits on is painted green like a parrot, which is Kama's vahana. Krishna is a romantic god, hence this association.

Isn't Hanuman the vahana of Rama?

Hanuman is Rama's bhakt, devotee, friend, brother, but not his vahana. The relationship between a vahana and god is very different. During the war in the Ramayana, Rama sometimes sits in a chariot sent by Indra or on Hanuman's shoulder, while Lakshmana sits on Angada's. There is a famous image where Hanuman is flying with Rama and Lakshmana seated on either shoulder, but he's not their vahana. In fact, Hanuman himself is considered a manifestation of Shiva.

Does any god or goddess have a completely weird, out-of-this-world vahana?

Kubera is the god of wealth and king of yakshas. He is known as Naravahana, one who has a human, nara, vehicle. While all other gods have animals as vehicles, Kubera travels on humans, which is strange.

The other one is Chamunda who has a terrifying form. She has scorpions all over her body and is known as pishacha or Preta Vahini as she travels on a bhoot, ghost, at night!

14

Ganga

People bathe in the Ganga to wash away their sins. Why is the Ganga considered so pure?

Hindus believe that the Ganga used to flow in Swarga where Amrita is found, and Amrita is said to have come to Bhu-loka in the form of Ganga. So the belief is that you will be absolved of your sins or achieve moksha if you bathe in her waters. Unless you consign the asthi, ashes, of the dead to the Ganga, they won't be able to travel across the Vaitarni river to Pitr-loka and be reborn. The Vaitarni separates Bhu-loka, the land of the living, from Pitr-loka, the land of the dead. Thus, the dead will remain stuck in Bhu-loka, as ghosts, and will suffer, achieving neither rebirth nor moksha.

Do the Vedas describe the Ganga?

Two rivers—Saraswati and Jahnavi—have been described in the Vedas, but the Saraswati appears to be important and is mentioned more frequently. Some historians believe that what's been written about in the Vedas is the Saraswati sabhyata, the civilization in India's north-west, from where people gradually moved towards the Ganga in north India. That was where Puranic Hinduism was born. This indicates a shift from the Vedas to the Puranas.

What does Ganga look like?

Ganga received a lot of attention during the Puranic period. You will see her idols at the doors of nearly every temple and beside city gates. She is described as a very beautiful woman, voluptuous and fecund, carrying a water pot, ghada, in one hand. She is also depicted in the symbol of Makara rashi, Capricorn. The makara, a sea creature with the tail of a fish and the head of an elephant, is her vehicle. Rationalists say the creature is probably the indigenous dolphin found in the Ganga, which is now an endangered species. There is confusion among some people between makara and magar, crocodile, so some folk images depict Ganga sitting on a crocodile.

Shiva and Ganga are supposed to have a very interesting relationship. Shiva is also known as Gangadhara, and Ganga is said to flow from his locks. Is Ganga Shiva's river then?

This is a contentious debate. Shaivas believe Ganga is their river and Vaishnavas believe she's theirs, because she is also called Vishnupadi, one who emerges from the feet of Vishnu. There is a story in which Vishnu, in his Vamana avatar, dwarf form, goes to Bali, the king of asuras, and asks for a boon allowing him to claim whatever land he can cover in three footsteps. Once the boon is granted, the Vamana becomes a giant, claiming Bhu-loka with one step and Swarga-loka with the next. When his foot extends into outer space, it happens to touch the Milky Way—what we call Akash Ganga—and the Ganga comes down to the earth with his foot. In another version of the story, when Vishnu raises his foot in space, Brahma is overcome with emotion. He pours water from his kamandal on to Vishnu's feet, which flows to earth as Ganga.

Shiva is Gangadhara because Ganga flows from his head and tresses, and Ganga is Vishnupadi because she is flowing from Vishnu's feet. These are the versions recounted in different traditions. A bit of the politics that happened during medieval times can be discerned here.

There is another fascinating story about Ganga. Shiva is known for his singing, although he rarely opens his mouth since he's a vairagi. Once, Shiva is singing and it's so beautiful that Vishnu literally melts and turns into water. Brahma collects this water in his kamandal, which is the Ganga.

It is said the Ganga is Shiva's wife—is that true?

There are some stories where Shiva has two wives, Gauri, or Parvati, and Ganga. They both are daughter of Parvat, the mountain. Folk tales say the two quarrel because one sits on Shiva's head and the other in his lap. In one story, Parvati, who is upset with Shiva, accuses him of keeping Ganga on his head and keeping her away. In response, Shiva embraces Parvati so tightly that they merge into one body and become Ardhanareshwara, the half-man, half-woman god. There are many such romantic stories about Shiva, Ganga and Gauri!

How did Ganga get her other name, Jahnavi? And also Bhagirathi?

When Ganga was descending to Bhu-loka, she was dancing gleefully and making a lot of noise. Rishi Jahanu got annoyed and drank the whole river up. Some say Jahanu was Shiva himself. Ganga then apologized for making so much noise and he released her through his ear. So she is also called Jahnavi, Jahanu's daughter.

Ganga's tributary is Bhagirathi. To try hard for something is to make a 'Bhagirath prayas', an oft-used phrase. Bhagirath was a Suryavanshi king whose ancestors had been cursed by Kapila Muni and turned into ash for disturbing his tapasya, meditation. Saddened by their fate, Bhagirath wondered if there was a chance that they might live again, be reborn, attain moksha, and so on. Kapila Muni told him they could be reborn only if their ashes were poured in the Ganga. For that, the Ganga would have to descend from heaven to earth. Bhagirath did tapasya and pleaded with the Ganga to come to earth. At long last Ganga agreed, but she said that the force of her fall would end up destroying the earth. Bhagirath then approached Shiva and requested him to hold the Ganga on his head. Shiva contained the force of the Ganga in his locks; Bhagirath was able to immerse the ashes of his ancestors in the river and they were reborn. The concept of rebirth is connected to getting another chance, because we aren't able to fulfil all our wishes in a single lifetime. Rebirth makes that second chance possible.

Does Ganga have siblings, family?

Ganga's sister is Yamuna. In many temples, Ganga and Yamuna are depicted beside each other. In images, Ganga is seated on a dolphin and Yamuna on a turtle. The dolphin is a leaping, fast-moving fish, whereas the turtle is slow. Similarly, the Ganga is fast, lively, full of cascades, while the Yamuna is slow and sluggish. Where Ganga is fair, almost white, like rapids, Yamuna is dark, and is thus also called Kalindi.

There are differences in their personalities as well. Ganga is restless, active, bubbly, even a bit manipulative; Yamuna is cheerless, fatigued and falls behind. Ganga is associated with Shiva, Yamuna with Vishnu, Krishna. One of Krishna's eight wives is Kalindi.

Yamuna is worshipped widely. The Srinathji temple in Rajasthan has a symbol of Yamuna in it, a ghada. Ganga and Yamuna never meet except at Prayag with an unseen river, the Saraswati. This sangam, the meeting place of the sisters, is the venue for the Kumbh Mela.

What is Dakshina Ganga?

India is called Jambudweep, a diamond-shaped land mass that appears like the jambul fruit. It is divided by the Vindhya mountains; the northern part is called Uttara-patha, and the southern, Dakshina-patha. The general understanding is that the Vedic tradition, with its beliefs and rituals, travelled from north to south. When the rishis travelled southwards, they needed a Ganga there too, thus the concept of Dakshina Ganga, or Ganga of the south.

The Kaveri river is often known as the Dakshina Ganga. One story is that when Rishi Agastya was travelling to the south, he carried Ganga water in his kamandal. While he was doing his tapasya, he kept the kamandal on a stone. Ganesha, in the form of a crow, came and tipped it over. The Kaveri river started to flow from the spot where the kamandal fell.

In another story, the Godavari river is Dakshina Ganga. This is a family-related story in the Godavari Mahatmya. Gauri or Parvati is unhappy with Ganga sitting on Shiva's head and wants to get rid of her. Once, Ganesha visits Rishi Gautama's ashram in the south in the form of a cow, and is wandering in his field of rice. The rishi throws a stone at the animal and Ganesha pretends to die. The rishi feels he has committed a sin, and must do penance. Ganesha reappears in his real form and, for his mother Parvati's happiness, tells the rishi to ask Shiva to send Ganga away from Kailasa. So, on Gautama's request Shiva sends Ganga there as Godavari.

In some stories, Ganga is Shiva's wife, in others she is Vishnu's wife, in yet others, she is unmarried. Can you clear this confusion?

This is a tough question to resolve. Ganga is an apsara, where aps is pani, water, which makes her the daughter of water. Ganga does not have a nath, that is, husband or lord. A river cannot be controlled. This is an important philosophical concept.

In stories, she is sometimes coupled with Shiva. In the Mahabharata, she is married to Shantanu. Shantanu happens to see her one day, falls in love with her beauty and proposes marriage. Ganga agrees to marry him on the condition that he will not restrict her freedom in any way. He agrees. In time, their first child is born, but Ganga drowns the newborn immediately. She does so with their next six children as well. When she is about to drown their eighth-born, Shantanu tries to stop her. She warns him that their marriage will be over if he goes back on his promise and questions her. Still, Shantanu demands an explanation. She tells him that their sons were the

Vasu who had resided in heaven in their previous birth. They had stolen Rishi Vasishtha's cow and he had cursed them, causing them to lose their place in heaven. Their atonement was to take birth on earth and be sent to Mrityu-loka, the land of the dead.

Ganga explains that she is drowning the children to secure the Vasu's release. Shantanu refuses to let her kill this child. Ganga says he'd be pushing the child into the painful cycle of birth and death. When Shantanu persists, she agrees to keep the infant alive and return him to his father later. She then disappears with the child.

In this unfortunate story, the child who survives is Bhishma, who ends up leading a rather tragic life. He doesn't get married, doesn't have children, doesn't even get to be king, and dies in a lot of pain. In his last moments, when Bhishma is lying on a bed of arrows, Ganga is grief-stricken even though she knows that is Bhishma's fate. She's aware of the facts of life and death, but as a mother she's overcome by emotion, and curses Arjuna, saying that his son will kill him the same way he has killed Bhishma, his foster father. Arjuna is a rare person who is cursed by Ganga—a passionate, impulsive goddess!

15

Gita

It is said the Gita is the most significant granth of the Hindus. Is that correct?

When we talk of the Gita what first comes to mind is the Bhagavad Gita that Krishna narrated to Arjuna before the war. But in the Mahabharata and the Puranas, there are many Gitas. Early in the Mahabharata, there is a Vyad Gita, or Butcher's Gita, where a butcher tells a Gita to a rishi. In the Shanti Parva, there is Pingala Gita where a prostitute is offering wisdom, and there is a Vichakshnu Gita where a Raja is doing the same. Gita basically means a conversation where learning is being imparted. It is written in a metre called Anustubh metre, which sounds musical while being read. Gita comes from geet, song.

So, how did the Gita become so important over time?

The Gita became important when the British East India Company first translated it into English 200 years ago. The Gita had never been translated before. While it was

written in Sanskrit 2000 years ago, Sanskrit scholars—
Adi Shankaracharya, Ramanujan, Madhavacharya,
Vallabhacharya—wrote commentaries on the Gita, called
Bhashyas, 1000 years ago. These too were in Sanskrit, so
only Brahmins could understand it.

During the fourteenth and fifteenth centuries, Bhakti
saints composed poems by simplifying the Gita and took
it to the common people through loka bhasha and loka
sangeet, colloquial language and folk songs. For instance,
Dyaneshwar has written in Marathi, Balaram Das in
Oriya, Annamacharya in Telugu, and so on. But the
exact and full translation was done by Charles Wilkins
in English. He was commissioned to do this, and he was
enthusiastic about it for a very interesting reason. Since
the Vedas had so many gods and goddesses, he thought
this religion was polytheistic and primitive, while the
Gita referred the most to one powerful deity and was
perhaps monotheistic. He felt the Gita was closer to the
Bible. And the British thought this book was better for the
Hindus.

Later, during the freedom struggle, most Indian leaders
read the Gita for the first time, and felt that this beautiful
text could unite the nation. On the one hand, Gandhi
found counsel for ahimsa in it and Lokmanya Tilak found
justification for righteous war. And on the other, Babasaheb
Ambedkar and D.D. Kosambi found elaboration of the caste
system in it and criticized the Gita. Many of those involved
in the freedom struggle expounded and wrote commentaries
on it. So, it is only in the last 300–400 years that the Gita
has acquired great importance. The way Christians have the
Holy Bible and Muslims have the Holy Quran, Hindus have
the Gita.

What is the structure of the Gita?

The Gita has 700 verses in eighteen chapters. The Mahabharata also has eighteen chapters, the war too was fought in eighteen days and eighteen armies were involved—seven of the Pandavas and eleven of the Kauravas. It's not clear why eighteen is significant, but we can speculate. Krishna calls our body Navadwarpur, the place with nine doors. These nine doors are the two eyes, the nose, two ears, the mouth, genitals and the anus. Any relationship between two people makes it eighteen doors, so when you're reading the Gita, maybe you've to think about this relationship.

Is the Gita related to the Vedas in any way?

Metaphorically, the Vedas are like the grass and the Upanishads are like the cows grazing on it. Krishna is the gwala, milkman, drawing milk from the cow, the milk being the Gita, which he gives to Arjuna. So the Bhagavad Gita can be called the *essence* of the Vedas.

What is the essence of the Gita?

Let me take you on a journey to answer this. Dhritarashtra asks about Kurukshetra: 'What is happening in this dharmakshetra, this land of dharma?' He asks what's going on between his sons and Pandu's sons? He does not refer to his nephews as his own but as 'Pandu's sons'. The demarcation between who is one's own and who is the *other* begins right from this moment. Sanjay, his sarathi, charioteer and servant, answers him, because he has been blessed with divya drishti, divine sight, by which he can see everything happening on the battlefield. He narrates what Duryodhana is saying. From the words Duryodhana uses, he seems nervous. He has eleven armies, and the support of Dronacharya, Bhishma and Karna. But seeing the Pandavas and their preparation makes him insecure; even though he has strength he is scared. On the other hand, when Arjuna sees the Kauravas, he thinks of both sides as his family. He questions why the two sides are fighting. There's a vast difference between Dhritarashtra and Arjuna. One thinks of the other side as paraye, separate, and the other considers all to be family.

This is why Arjuna receives the learning of the Gita. He wonders about the origin of the divide between the two sides. A big doubt arises in his mind: How can there be dharma in killing his own family? How can such a war be fought? To resolve this dilemma, he goes to Krishna. At first, Krishna tells him simply that the Kauravas took your territory, humiliated your wife, treated you all badly, are unwilling to negotiate or compromise for peace, and so on. But Arjuna is unconvinced; he still feels it's not right to cause so much bloodshed and wants to drop everything. All Krishna's positive and negative arguments, his pleas, and even the insinuation that Arjuna is being unmanly, fail to move the Pandava warrior.

Then, the second chapter onwards, Krishna's tone changes. He says no one is going to die here, everyone is immortal. Arjuna is taken aback. Krishna says life and death are illusions. Then he goes deeper into the concept. The soul can never be cut into pieces by any weapon, he says, nor can it be burned by fire, moistened by water, or withered by the wind. We believe what we see is the truth. But the truth is much larger. It extends beyond the horizon that we see—a world we don't know about. We feel our life, this life, is the only one there is. Like we claim we will change the world in our lifetimes. Krishna says that's never going to happen. Life is a flowing river in which you too are flowing. Krishna thus changes the canvas of the story.

Then he focuses on karma. There are two words that are key—yagya and yog. Yagya is exchange or relationship. In life, you have to give and take; even when you don't actively do anything, an exchange is going on. Yog is connection, while viyog is disconnection. There are connections between all kinds of things—a person's with another person, a person's with his heart, mind, body, and so on. So, there's a connection with the soul inside and with others outside. Jeevatma is inside and paramatma, outside. Jeeva is the self, while para is others; this story is about the self and others. If you run away, you'll be running away from paramatma. Arjuna now displays nervousness and says that nobody can control the mind. Even if he were to try, he says, after a while it would escape his grasp.

Krishna changes tack again and becomes like a parent dealing with a frightened child. He takes on an emotional tone and says that when you don't have any support, your support is God, Bhagavan. For the Arjuna who is at sea, he brings a rescue boat, saying, 'Don't worry, whatever happens I'll be with you.' When Arjuna asks him what he means by 'I will be with you', Krishna shows him his real form—the Virat-Swarup, the larger-than-life form. Here, for the first time in the Gita, in the middle of it, God is described. It is a beautiful, detailed description—Krishna says he is the mountain, he is the elements, chara, achara, deva, asura, king, beggar, everything.

The middle chapters of the Gita are basically giving confidence to a scared man. Anyone can give advice, but a person cannot act, cannot do his karma, unless he is confident. Krishna realizes that Arjuna is nervous and reassures him that he has his support. And unlike these days when we try to teach right at the beginning, it is only towards the end, only when Arjuna calms down, that Krishna imparts wisdom. And the conversation that follows is sophisticated.

Among living beings, humans are unique, because animals and other creatures run after food. Humans search for meaning. Krishna says we don't need validation from anyone outside us. The meaning is inside. We are alive so we have meaning, we are valid. Inside us there is atma. But we forget that and seek meaning in another's viewpoint. This gives birth to aham, ego, which makes us want praise, respect from someone outside. Thus we are trapped in the indrajaal, the web of the senses, that is, the illusory material world.

Krishna tells Arjuna, 'If you are seeking validation from outside you, if you are hoping that others will praise what a great warrior you are, then you are finished. But if you are working from within, for your inner peace and satisfaction, then do whatever you want. Why do you not want to fight? Because people will say you fought your family? Whatever is meant to happen will happen. There is no certainty that you will win, nor that you will lose. Why are you so tense? Don't expect to be perfect. Nobody is, including me. Don't run after accolades. Just do your karma.'

This is the essence of the Gita.

Does Krishna directly tell Arjuna to kill the Kauravas?

No, Krishna never tells him this. There is in fact a shloka which says, 'Do as you wish.' In Hinduism, no specific instructions are ever given. Karma is entirely yours: action, its reaction, its repercussion—you have to take responsibility for it all. Another person's advice does not matter. These days, in popular depictions of the Mahabharata, Krishna is shown as a politician who manipulates everyone. But they don't see what happens at the end of the war—the line of the Kurus is destroyed, all the sons of the Pandavas die, and even the Yadus are destroyed. What does he stand to gain from any of it? This had to happen.

The Gita is about making Arjuna understand why he is fighting this war. Like two dogs fighting over a bone, the two families are fighting over land. If the Pandavas don't fight, what will they eat—it's a war for their survival. This is why for them it's a dharma yudh, righteous war, whereas for the Kauravas it's an adharma yudh, because they are fighting merely for pride and power. It is their insecurity that is making them do this. But Krishna doesn't ever overtly state this. He leaves it for Arjuna to realize. Hindu religion will never give clear instructions. In the Vedas, it is repeatedly emphasized that all responsibility lies with oneself—you cannot blame anyone else for what happens to you. You have come into this world alone, you will live and die alone, and will be amar, immortal, alone.

Tell us a lesser-known story about the Gita.

In the Ashwamedha Parva of the Mahabharata, Yudhishtira conducts an Ashwamedha yagna and establishes his authority over the kingdom. Krishna counsels everyone and is about to leave the palace when Arjuna comes up to him and says he can't remember the sermon Krishna had given him before the war. It's funny in a way and has a very human touch. Krishna too doesn't expect much from Arjuna in this regard. For him Arjuna is like his calf.

In fact, Krishna is sometimes called a cow, and in the Dyaneshwar Gita, he is known as Vithai. In Marathi, his name is Lord Vitthal, so Vithai means Mother Krishna. Like a mother, he too indulges Arjuna and explains the lesson to him again. As the body keeps being reborn, for many subsequent lives, and the cycle continues, so will Krishna keep imparting the lesson. At some point the lesson will be understood or moksha achieved—there is no hurry as time is eternal!

Can we get the knowledge of the Gita without knowing Sanskrit?

There is no language for knowledge. Knowledge is nirgun, formless; language is sagun, with form. Bhasha, language, is like a container in which you pour water. A good container helps you grasp the water better. But ultimately, you want the water, not the container. I focus on the knowledge, not the language.

What for you is the most interesting concept in the Gita?

For me it is the concept of yog, that is, connections. How human beings connect to each other. In the Mahabharata, there is no hero or villain. They are all human beings, acting out of their insecurities. There are some good actions, some condemnable. But when you think along the concept of yog, connect with them, you will not judge them, rather you will see through their failings. This is the knowledge you gain.

16

Pilgrimage

In India, why do people go on tirth yatras, pilgrimages?

People everywhere go on tirth yatras. Perhaps there is a psychological reason for it. In our predominantly agricultural society, people live in one village all their lives. Tirth yatras were probably the rishis' way of encouraging them to expand their boundaries, their minds. Travelling brings experience and wisdom. Yatra is a concept in all religions. For instance, Muslims undertake the Haj pilgrimage to Mecca.

There is a brahmacharya yatra in which children go to a gurukul to learn from a teacher. It's like a boarding school, where they live until their minds are opened to learning. Vanaprasth ashrama is when old people leave their home and go to a vana, forest. People may also take sanyas and go on yatra with the idea of never returning home, leaving the householder's life behind. After a wedding, a woman goes in a doli to her new home. This is also a yatra. The only other yatra she can take, it is said, is when her body travels from her husband's home to the cremation ground. To escape this regulated world, a tirth yatra came into being. We are all koopmandukas, frogs in a well. We feel our world is the only world there is. Travel expands that world view.

In the Sama Veda, there are two kinds of songs—of the grama, village, and the aranya, forest. The grama songs usually say, go to the forest and come back: the suggestion is to experience a wild place where there are no rules, laws, morals; see for yourself what prakriti, nature, is and return. So, in the Buddha Charitra, Buddha embarks on a yatra to seek answers. He goes as Prince Siddhartha, and returns as Buddha after receiving enlightenment. Although we see Rama residing in the forest for his vanavas, it is actually a yatra. In the Mahabharata too there is a yatra.

Do our shastras mention tirth yatras?

Yes. When the Pandavas are exiled to the jungle for thirteen years they wonder what they will do with all that time—they worry that they'll get bored! Krishna suggests they go on a tirth yatra. This is the first mention of a tirth yatra, 2000 years ago, when the Mahabharata was composed. Our texts say, go to the mountains, rivers, ponds—keep travelling. The Pandavas were probably the first tirth yatris.

What does tirth mean?

These days, the water given to bhakts, devotees, after it has been offered to god at temples, is called tirth. But there is a detailed meaning. To cross a river, one has to take a boat. But sometimes the river is so shallow that one can simply walk across. That is a ford, which is known as tirth. Tirth is crossing from one bank to the other without help. It's a physical concept; rishis must've looked for tirths to be able to cross over. Psychologically, it means achieving a state of nirgun, that which is formless, nameless, the world of atma or paramatma. In Jainism, God is called Tirthankara, one who is able to find tirth, and achieve mukti, release, from samsaric, material, life; he also shows the way to achieve it. Nowadays, tirth has come to mean a pilgrim spot, which can be a temple or a mountain where people go to express their devotion.

Tell us about Vishnu's char dham.

The concept of the char dham, four pilgrimage spots, has become popular in the last 1000 years. Adi Shankaracharya, a prominent guru of Vedanta, had a major contribution in establishing Hinduism. He set up four maths, monasteries, in four corners of India. One is at Badrikapuri in the Himalayas where Vishnu does tapasya in the form of Nara-Narayana under a ber, badri, tree. The second is at Jagannath Puri in Odisha where Vishnu has bhog, that is, eats. The world's largest pressure cooker is here. Every day an enormous quantity of food is prepared and offered to the gods, and later sold at Anand Bazar. Third is the Rameshwaram temple in Tamil Nadu, where Vishnu bathes. The fourth is Dwarka, in Gujarat, where Vishnu, as Krishna, is king.

Tell us about the twelve jyotirlingas of Shiva.

Yes. Every village has a Shiva-linga somewhere or the other, not necessarily in a temple as Shiva is a vairagi. It could be outside the village, under a tree, near a cremation ground, anywhere. Adi Shankaracharya identified twelve specific sites all across India, where Shiva had first appeared in his svayambhu roop, that is, when he created himself. In the Puranas, it is said that he appeared as an agni-stambh, pillar of fire, before his devotees. Some of these sites are Kedarnath in Uttarakhand; Kashi Vishwanath in Uttar Pradesh; Mahakaleshwar in Ujjain, Madhya Pradesh; Trimbakeshwar and Bhimashankar in Maharashtra; Srisailam in Andhra Pradesh where he is worshipped as Mallikarjun; and Rameshwaram in Tamil Nadu. There are big temples in many other places as well, like Babulnath in Mumbai and the famous Bhairava temple in Delhi. But Adi Shankaracharya identified these twelve jyotirlingas as important points for Shaivas, like the char dham are for Vaishnavas.

And there are Shakti peeths for Devi followers?

There is a story where Daksha Prajapati's daughter Sati is married to Shiva. Daksha and Shiva do not get along since the former is too rigidly ritualistic and Shiva does not care about rules because he is a vairagi. Once, Daksha Prajapati organizes a yagna to which he does not invite Shiva. Sati feels so hurt, she invokes Agni and burns herself. An angry Shiva destroys the yagna shala, and chops off Daksha Prajapati's head. When he finally calms down, he gives the king a new head, hoists Sati's dead body on to his shoulder and roams around the Brahmanda, weeping in sorrow. This is the first time Shiva experiences pain.

Life on the planet comes to a standstill. Vishnu says this cannot go on. With his Sudarshan chakra, he cuts Sati's body into many parts. The places where these parts fell are Shakti peeths. Her foot is said to have fallen in Kolkata, tongue in Jwalamukhi in Himachal Pradesh. Tara Tarini temples are in the east, south, west; somewhere there are eyes (Naina Devi), elsewhere hands, feet, ears. The idea is probably that all of India is Sati's severed body and there is some part of her everywhere.

An interesting theory is that the British gave us a map for the country and created India, but that's not entirely true. Basically, it is the tirth yatris who have mapped the geography of India. Our land is connected by tirths, be it by rivers, ponds, mountains, confluences (like Kashi), and it is amidst all these that towns gradually developed. In towns emerged bazaars, where traders came, who were entertained by nat, street performers, accompanied by prostitutes, and so on. These sites became cultural zones, where people assembled from different places from time to time. The permanent members of these towns were the priests and prostitutes. So our country is made of all these travels.

Is there a tirth yatra for Ganesha?

There is a famous one for him in Maharashtra, known as Ashtavinayaka, literally, eight gods. There are eight Ganesha temples here. In the seventeenth and eighteenth centuries, the Peshwas ruled the region. They worshipped Ganesha, who was their ishta-devata, household deity. Pune was their capital around which these temples exist. It is said your prayers will be answered if you visit them.

Like the char dham, the Shakti peeths, the jyotirlingas, which are known all across the country, in each region there are specific yatras that are locally popular, like the Ashtavinayaka in Maharashtra. Another famous one was started by the Vaishnavas there, like Dyaneshwar and Tukaram, who were part of the Maharashtra dharma and started the Varkari sect. In their yatra, thousands of Varkaris go to Pandharpur to worship Vitthal, Krishna, during the rainy season, chaumas, every year.

Are there other yatras that are not very well known?

Usually people of the north don't know about the yatras of the south, and vice versa. In Tamil Nadu, there is a yatra for Murugan, Kartikeya, Shiva's son, in the Palani hills where there are seven or eight temples. Long ago, Tamil Chettiyar merchants travelled to Malaysia where they established a special Murugan shrine at the famous Batu Caves. Malaysia is an Islamic country, but it is relatively secular. So every year, there is a big Thaipusam festival during which Tamilians worship at the Murugan shrine. Sometimes, yatris too form a tirth yatra.

Why are devotees of Vaishno Devi expected to stop by at the Bhairava temple on their way back from their tirth?

The Vaishno Devi temple is in Jammu. Unlike other devis, she is a vegetarian. There's a Ramayana-related story. There was a lady called Vedavati who wanted to marry Rama. He said he was monogamous and could not marry her in this yuga, but he promised to do so in another yuga. So she sat in tapasya there, waiting for Rama. Once, to test her, a Tantric sadhu called Bhairava arrives and asks for food. When she serves him, he says he wants tantric, physical, food. She says that is impossible as she belongs to Rama. When he tries to force her, she runs away and Bhairava chases after her. She flees through many caves, but at one point she suddenly turns around and angrily cuts off Bhairava's head. As he's dying, he asks for her forgiveness. She forgives him and tells him that, henceforth, anyone who came for her darshan would visit him as well.

At most tirth yatras, one temple is always connected with another. It is said your yatra will not bear fruit unless you visit the other one. At Tirupati (Vaishnava tradition), they'll say you must visit Kalahasti (Shaiva tradition). Similarly, Vaishno Devi is of Shakta tradition and Bhairava of Shaiva. These are attempts made by different traditions to connect with each other.

When did the tirth yatra for Sai Baba become popular?

Shirdi's Sai Baba is about 100 years old; we can even see his photographs. In India, we worship gurus and sants, not only gods and goddesses. Shirdi's Sai Baba is popular with all communities and religions. Some say he became famous because he was featured in the Hindi film, *Amar Akbar Anthony*! We can't say for sure, but if people begin to worship someone, he becomes god. God creates devotees, and devotees too create gods.

What is the significance of the Sabarimala yatra in the south?

Sabari is a tribe and malay is a mountain. Only men can go on this yatra, after taking an oath of brahmacharya, celibacy, and wearing black clothes—these are strict rules. The mountain has eighteen steep steps. There is an Ayyappa temple here, in Kerala. Another name for him is Hariharasuta. In Kerala (earlier called Chera Pradesh) there was a king, Rajasekhara Pandiyan, who was childless. He prayed to Shiva and Vishnu for a child. Shiva gave him his own son, Hariharasuta. The king gave him two names—Ayyappan and Manikandana. After his arrival, the queen too gave birth to a boy. She began to favour her own son and plotted to kill Ayyappan. She told him she was unwell and needed a tigress's milk. Ayyappan went to the forest and came back riding a tiger, with the milk. He also killed a rakshasi, Mahishi, in the forest. Everyone said he should become king. But he knew that his mother did not want that so he said he'd become a yogi instead, stay unmarried and sit on a mountain. Sabarimala is that mountain where every year the yatra takes place.

Can you tell us about the Kavad yatra?

The Kavad yatra happens in the month of Shravana when the boys from the village go to the Ganga and bring the water back in a ghada, pot, to pour on to the Shiva-linga. The pots are balanced from a kavad, a beam with a basket hanging from each end, held on the shoulder. It is in a kavad that Shravana Kumar carried his blind parents. The rule is that the pots should not be kept on the floor until they reach the temple. On the way, many preparations are done for the Kavad, where they can suspend their kavads from a tree or poles. The kavad is beautifully decorated, with colourful flags, string, golden festoons, etc. In the south too, this yatra is popular for Murugan, and there they decorate the kavads with peacock feathers.

The kavad is associated with grihasthi, the household, suggesting to Shiva that you'll have to lift the weight of the world.

17

Gods and Food

Why is anna, food, accorded so much importance in our culture?

In Yoga-shastra, our body is called annakosha, that is, flesh formed from anna. Our flesh then becomes food for other animals. All living beings need anna for their annakosha. Plants eat the elements, especially the five major ones, the pancha mahabhut, including sunlight and water. Plants, in turn, are consumed by animals, which are then eaten by other animals. Humans eat both plants and animals. Food and the action of eating maintain life; life eats life.

The Upanishads give a lot of importance to food. Without food, the world cannot exist. We can discuss atma, meaning, talk of high intellectual and spiritual matters, but at the most practical level, 'anna hi satya hai'— food is truth. It is emphasized in the texts to remind us about the meaning of existence. Anna is called Brahmin, the way bhasha is called Brahmin. God resides in food; the one who eats is God, what you are eating is also God. The concept that 'God is life and life is food' is repeated constantly in mantras and other texts so that we don't forget the importance of food.

The bhog offered to the gods is mostly milk and fruit. Are these their favourite foods or is there some other reason behind it?

You can take this literally or metaphorically. The earth is known as Vasundhara, that which holds up vasu, or plants. So if the earth is a cow, plants are its milk. In the Vedas, milk is given a lot of importance. Ghee, a milk product, is offered during yagnas to Agni, said to be the hunger of the gods. Panchamruta contains five milk products—milk, both raw and boiled, ghee, butter and yoghurt. Go-ras, cow urine, honey and jaggery are all mixed in and offered to the gods. In the Puranas, it is said that Vishnu lies on Kshir Sagar, an ocean of milk. So, nature, prakriti, is visualized as an ocean of milk. Whatever you get from nature is like milk—that's the analogy. Which is why gods are always offered milk.

Fruit may be raw or ripe. All fruits have different tastes, and are offered to the gods depending on the type of fruit. Devis are given sour and spicy fruits. Lakshmi is offered amlas, the Indian gooseberry, lemon and chillies. Vishnu is given sweet fruits. Shiva is given dry fruits perhaps because they're found in cooler climes, or because rishis carried them when they journeyed.

What are the favourite foods of Shiva and Vishnu?

One way of looking at it is that Shiva is a vairagi, a tapasvi who wishes to stay away from domestic life, while Vishnu, in the form of Rama or Krishna, lives a householder's life. So Shiva is offered raw unprocessed milk and Vishnu, processed milk products like butter and ghee. Shiva is content with whatever is available. But because Vishnu is a householder, his offerings require effort; he needs manufactured products. To extract the butter from the milk, you have to put in a lot of work, or you will not see results. A lot of value is accorded to shram, labour. So, typically, Vishnu is offered cooked food. During the Annakuta festival around Diwali, Krishna is offered a mountain of food, the chhappan bhog, or fifty-six items— because food is extremely important for a householder. The food offered matches the lifestyle of the god.

Do only gods like bhog; do goddesses not like it?

For devis, traditionally, there would be blood sacrifices— goats, buffaloes, birds. These days it is not popular because of animal rights. A devi is Raktavilasini, one who loves rakt, blood. We can take it literally, but there is a metaphorical aspect to it. Bhudevi, the earth goddess, is considered to be a cow whose milk sustains everyone. But how will she sustain herself? In the form of Gauri, she gives milk, and in the form of Kali, she drinks blood—the cycle of life, as it were. This is to emphasize the idea that whenever you eat, you've killed something, sacrificed someone, offered bali.

Plant food comes from farms which were created after decimating forests, destroying mountains and rivers, killing countless creatures in the process. The Devi always reminds you that to build your civilization, sanskriti, you destroy prakriti, nature. And so she demands blood, even narabali, human sacrifice. In the Bhagavata Purana, Bhudevi tells Vishnu that people are troubling her and she wants to drink their blood. In fact, the secret reason behind the wars in the

Ramayana and the Mahabharata is that Bhudevi is thirsty. There has been too much adharma, immorality, and man has exploited her terribly, and now she wants blood in return. So, in the form of Rama and Krishna, Vishnu makes the wars happen. These are a kind of narabali. There is a story in the Mahabharata in which Arjuna and Bhima are quarrelling about who showed greater prowess during the war. They are told that there is a head atop a mountain who can give them the answer since he observed the entire war from up there. Some say the head's name was Barbarika, others say it is Arvan. The head said, 'I don't know any Kaurava, Pandava, or great warrior. I only saw Bhudevi, in the form of Kali, drinking the blood of all the warriors as Vishnu's Sudarshan chakra decimated them.'

Lakshmi, the goddess of wealth, has a sister, Alakshmi, the goddess of feuds—both may enter a house together. In Mumbai, there's a common custom of hanging a lemon and seven chillies above the threshold as an offering to Alakshmi, so that she can partake of it and remain outside the house. Inside the house, sweet bhog is offered to invite Lakshmi in.

Is there any specific story regarding bhog in the Ramayana or the Mahabhrata?

In Ayodhya, there's a place known as Sita's kitchen. Sita was a very good cook. And Draupadi was famous for her generosity. Nobody went hungry from her kitchen. During their stay in the forest, after being exiled from the palace, the Pandavas don't have anything. Draupadi feels bad that she won't be able to feed whoever comes to her door. To tease her, Duryodhana sends Durvasa and some other rishis to her. They ask her for food. She requests them to go and bathe in the river, while she prepares a meal for them. Once they depart, she goes inside and starts weeping in despair.

It is then that Krishna arrives. He says there must be something that she can offer the rishis. Dismayed, Draupadi shows him the empty vessels, saying that she'd fed her husbands and then eaten whatever little remained. Krishna picks up one leftover grain of rice and eats it. He is satiated and because of that, so are the rishis. They, in turn, feel they will end up disrespecting Draupadi if they don't eat anything she offers, so they make a hasty exit. This is how Krishna protects Draupadi's dignity.

However, Krishna tells Draupadi to pray to Surya, the sun god, for a solution to her problem. Draupadi does so and Surya gives her a thali, plate. There's a phrase 'Draupadi ki thali', which is similar to the concept of 'mataji ka bhandar', implying that there will always be food in the kitchen. Each day, Draupadi's thali stayed full until she ate. She would feed hundreds of people and be the last to eat. But once she had eaten, there would be no more food till the next day.

In these stories, there are no male cooks. How is that possible?

There are such references in the Mahabharata. Nala is a powerful, handsome and rich king, married to beautiful Damayanti, and their life goes well. Later, due to unfortunate circumstances, they become so poor that Nala has to become a servant to another king, and cook for him. This story is more famous in Kerala. According to the Malayalam Mahabharata, the world's greatest cook is Nala. Even now, when you find a good male cook, he's compared to Nala.

I've heard that people offer betel leaf, paan, to the gods. Why?

Offering paan and supari, betel nut, is an Indian tradition. At
the end of a meal, you eat paan–supari, which indicates all is
well with your life, and that you are prosperous and content.
It is a sign of a happy grihastha jeevan, household life. This is
offered only to married gods, never to Shiva.

In some images, Lakshmi offers paan to Vishnu. It's a sign
of ayyashi, merrymaking, and of luxury, success and happiness.
And we want all these in our lives.

What is shriphal?

Shri is Lakshmi, phal is fruit. It's a fruit that you get round the
year and one which is easily available. These are fruit which
generate on their own, and don't require too much effort, like
coconuts or bananas. These are always kept in the thali for
puja. Not only are these nutritious, but they are also a symbol
of endless wealth and affluence.

Sometimes rice is also called shriphal. Under a kalash,
pot, for a puja, you spread rice, and a coconut is placed on
the mouth of the kalash. These are signs of Lakshmi. They
are found in abundance, and there will be prosperity wherever
they are.

18

Eras

Everywhere we look or hear, something bad is happening. Do you think we are now living in the Kali Yuga?

In every age, or yuga, people feel they are living through the worst times. Older people have a tendency to say that things were better in their childhood, and are clearly worsening now. There are two schools of thought—one says we are progressing and the world is improving, while the other believes the world is in decline.

We should take the concept of Kali Yuga as a metaphor, rather than thinking that doomsday is round the corner! Philosophically, we can say that everything except God is ever-changing. God is nitya, permanent, while the rest is impermanent, anitya, and therefore destructible, nashwar. The concept of time is cyclical—it come and goes. In Hindi, kal is the word for both yesterday and tomorrow. This concept is present in Jainism too, where the cyclical nature of time is compared to the zigzag movement of a snake. Good times are called Uttasarpini, bad times are called Avasarpini. There are further divisions in this. Time is like a wave—at the crest is shusham shusham (good), thereafter on the lower stroke is shusham dusham, the trough is dusham dusham (bad), then dusham shusham on the upward stroke and back to shusham shusham. Same in Hinduism. Since nothing is permanent, neither is Kali Yuga.

How many yugas do we have, and which are these?

Yuga is a method of dividing time, to make sense of the infinity of time. Scientists disagree; they claim that there was a definite beginning in the form of the Big Bang. But, according to the shastras, time is eternal and has neither beginning nor end. To control it, human beings have to divide it.

Traditionally, one day is considered from sunrise to sunset. There are four prahars during the day, and four during the night. The importance of the number four is interesting. Four is a solid geometrical number. There are four corners in a house, four directions, four varnas or castes and four ashrams or stages of life. The varnas are Brahmin, Kshatriya, Vaishya, Shudra. The ashrams are brahmacharya or student life, grihastha or married life, vanaprastha or retired life and sanyasa or hermitic life after renunciation. Cosmic time too has been divided into four eras—Satya or Krita Yuga, Treta Yuga, Dvapara Yuga, Kali Yuga followed by pralaya or complete devastation and then the cycle begins anew with Satya Yuga. The four yugas together form a manavatar or kalpa. However, prakriti, nature, doesn't work according to yugas. It has seasons, ritu, which come and go. Yugas are a concept in sanskriti, culture.

Similar to the division of our lives by age groups, everything in culture, like society, organizations, even the growth of a company, has four phases. There's innocence at the start-up stage, stability, growth and decay. I feel it's more about culture (sanskriti) than about the universe (samsara).

How do we know when the changeover from one yuga to another takes place?

One way of understanding this is to view dharma as a cow with four legs. In Krita Yuga it has four legs. When one leg decays (moral degeneration), she becomes lame and the Treta Yuga begins. During the Dvapara Yuga, she stands on just two legs after a second leg has decayed, and in the Kali Yuga, the cow is standing on just one leg. When the fourth leg is gone, pralaya is upon the world.

Another interesting belief is that when Vishnu sleeps, there's pralaya. He wakes up and the Krita Yuga begins. Then his avatars appear—Rama in the Treta Yuga, Krishna in the Dvapara Yuga. Eventually, he gets tired in Kali Yuga and goes to sleep. Creation occurs when Vishnu awakens and pralaya when he sleeps.

When Vishnu sleeps, who looks after the Brahmanda, the cosmos?

Yuga is associated with sanskriti, not prakriti, which is timeless. Prakriti existed before sanskriti and will continue to after as well. We've given the form of Devi to prakriti. When Vishnu awakens, sanskriti awakens. In the Puranas, it is said that when Vishnu sleeps, Yoganidra manages or guards the universe. Devi is always there. When Vishnu wakes up, Yogamaya, another form of Yoganidra, takes her place and outsources her work to him!

Which yugas were Rama and Krishna born in?

The Ramayana and the Mahabharata are the stories of two yugas—Treta and Dvapara. Everything is okay in Krita Yuga. The coming of Parashurama signals the end of that yuga. Rama's arrival marks the end of the Treta Yuga, and Krishna's, the end of Dvapara. And perhaps Kalki's arrival will mark the end of Kali Yuga. You can take this literally or metaphorically. In the Krita Yuga, there were no rules or customs, niti and riti, because humans were so honest and generous. In Parashurama's story, a theft happens for the first time. A cow given to Jamadagni is stolen. That's when the age of rules begins. With rules came the maryada purushottam, one who respects rules. The famous line in the Tulsidas Ramayana, 'prana jaaye par vachan na jaaye'—life can be sacrificed to keep one's word—shows the importance of Raghukul niti, where Rama's (Raghu) society followed rules. It was an innocent age.

In the Dvapara Yuga, the confusion starts. Even by following the rules, adharma, immorality, can exist. In fact, rules are made an instrument of adharma. Bhishma and Drona follow the rules and yet the Pandavas suffer. Nobody loves, nobody gives generously. In the Kali Yuga, neither niti nor riti is respected. No one knows what dharma or adharma is; there are unending debates on this, but no resolution. This strange world is known as Kali Yuga, and who's to say whether we're in it or if it's yet to come.

What is the story of Shiva? How and in which yuga was he born?

A life can be calculated in time with birth and death. Yonija is one born from the womb, yoni. Rama was born to Kaushalya,

Krishna to Devaki. Rama dies by walking into the Sarayu river; Krishna is injured by an arrow shot by Jara, an archer, that leads to his death. So they have experienced birth, life which death. There is a world beyond this, that of ayonija or svayambhu, where the beings create themselves. There is no old age or death here; this is the nitya or permanent world, the world of the gods. In Jainism it is called Siddha-loka, land of the siddhas, realized souls. Shiva and Vishnu belong in this world. Here, they are always young, and there is no autumn, no winter, there's always spring, happiness. Nor is there death, fear, hunger.

There are two worlds—one permanent, the other impermanent, where time is cyclical in the form of changing yugas. There's an interesting dialogue in Valmiki's Ramayana about cyclical time. When Rama asks Sita to stay back instead of accompanying him into the forest, she refuses. Her clinching argument is, 'I go with you in every Ramayana, why are you stopping me in this one?' It's as though she is aware that the Ramayana has happened before. In folklore, this occurs in the story of Hanuman's mudrika, ring.

The god of time tells Rama that his duty on earth is over, and he should accept death and return to his heavenly abode, Vaikuntha. Rama is willing to invite Yama, the god of death, but knows that his steadfast devotee Hanuman will not let him come anywhere near Rama. To distract Hanuman, Rama drops his ring in a crevice and asks Hanuman to bring it back. Hanuman instantly shrinks and dives into the crevice. He travels very far underground and reaches Naga-loka, land of serpents, where he meets the naga king Vasuki. He asks for his help in finding Rama's ring. Vasuki directs him to a mountain. As he nears it, Hanuman realizes that it's a mountain of rings. How will I find Rama's ring in this, he wonders. Vasuki tells him that they are all Rama's rings, that it's a timeless story in which a vanara comes looking for Rama's ring during which time Rama dies on earth. That's when the Treta Yuga ends. This cycle has been going on since time immemorial. Hanuman understands that the cycle of birth, death, rebirth cannot be stopped and will always go on.

This story shows Hanuman's—and, by extension, our—failings. Hanuman is strong and powerful, but is scared of death. He doesn't want Rama to leave him. This story is for Hanuman to learn a lesson, that every being who is born will die and will be reborn. This cycle will go on eternally. Philosophically, the concept is that this life we are living has been lived before by us and will be repeated. The world changes, and yet does not change. You can't change the world, but you can improve the way you meet the same challenges and manage the world. The most important lesson of Indian philosophy is control over our minds. Just as Hanuman couldn't stall the flow of time and prevent Rama from dying, you cannot control the world. But once you accept the reality of death, you'll suffer less and be able to live to the fullest.

When did the Kali Yuga begin? Can you pinpoint an exact date?

One should not take ancient or religious texts literally. For instance, according to the Bible the world began exactly 5000 years ago. One has to understand the essence of these texts, which is that nothing is permanent. Everything has a positive time and a negative time. Everything is in transition. The way our childhood ends, so does the Krita Yuga; the way our youth comes to an end, so does grihastha ashram, and so on. To pinpoint a date, say, for Rama's birth, is to lose the real meaning behind the story. I focus on the spirit, not the letter, of what has been said.

19

Creation

According to the Puranas, how was srishti, the universe, created?

Between the Vedas that came 4000 years ago and the Puranas that came 2000 years ago, there were the Brahmanas and Aranyakas. All of these texts contain various stories of creation. The Vedas have a creation hymn called Nasadiya Sukta, and in it we come to see the sophistication of the Vedic period. The poet says, what came first—jal (water) or sthal (land), light or darkness, summer or winter, who took the first breath, and so on. Then he says, maybe the gods created, but then who created the gods, because they came later? Perhaps the gods know the mystery, and perhaps they too don't. This is all speculation; there are no clear answers.

But, the poet says, for anything to be created in the universe, it must be preceded by desire. So, if desire is the seed, then the cosmos is its fruit. The Atharva Veda says kama came first—not Kama, the god of love, that we know, but kama itself, desire. The Yajur Veda mentions a Purushamedha yagna, and that the world is Prajapati. When Prajapati was sacrificed, the

131

world came into being. From Prajapati's head came Brahmins, from his hands, Kshatriyas, from his stomach, Vaniks, and from his feet, Shudras. One living being was torn to form samaj, society. The Vedas are made up of samhitas (collections of mantras), Brahmanas (which contain details of yagnas) and Aranyakas (on philosophical thought). The Upanishads discuss the Vedas. So the umbrella term Vedas includes these various texts; the Nasadiya Sukta is from a samhita.

In the aranyaka (forest), Prajapati (father of all beings) sees a woman, Shatarupa (one who has many roops). He is attracted to her and pursues her. She takes different feminine forms, and he takes the corresponding male forms. When she is a cow, he becomes a bull; when she turns into a mare, he becomes a horse, and so on. This is how all animals come into being, from elephants to ants. This is one story.

Gradually, the name of Manu begins to appear in our texts and the idea that he created the universe. He married Shatarupa and started the human race. There are many such stories in all the different texts, but no single fixed story.

Since Brahma is known as the creator, how did he create the universe?

Brahma created the cosmos, or Brahmanda, that is Brahma's egg. From Brahma's mind were formed the Manasputras. First were born four Sanat-Kumars, who said they were not interested in srishti so would become sanyasis. Then he begot the Sapta Rishis, seven rishis, who said they'd need women to procreate. So Brahma created a woman and gave each rishi a wife. Thus were all living beings born. Famous among these rishis is Kashyapa, which means turtle. He is father to Adityas or devas (from wife Aditi), Daityas or asuras (from wife Diti),

Danavas (from Danus), nagas (from Kadru), birds (from Vinata), fish (from Timi). This is the most common story associated with Brahma.

What is the story in the Shaiva tradition?

At the beginning was the hiranyagarbha (golden womb), which was in the shape of a lotus. The word hiranyagarbha is there in the Vedas as well. When it bloomed, Brahma was in it. He saw a vision of Ardhanareshwara, that is, Shiva as half-woman, half-man, and inspired by it he created srishti. From the man he created Manu and from the woman, Shatarupa. In another version, Shiva divides himself into Shiva and Shakti. From Shiva arose men, nara, and women, mada, from Shakti.

And in the Vaishnava tradition?

The Vaishnava tradition has elaborate stories. Some of these stories are found in the Brahmanas, and they evolved later. The most popular story is that everything was asleep in the beginning. Then Vishnu wakes up, starts breathing, and his desires are awakened. From his navel grows a lotus, in which Brahma is seated. When the lotus blooms, Brahma opens his eyes. Seeing no other life he gets frightened. His fear is so great that he feels he'll have to create another being so he's not alone. This fear is mentioned in the Brihadaranyaka Upanishad as well—that creation began with fear. The first being is scared of loneliness and needs company, and so he creates a woman, is attracted by her, and the Brahmanda is formed.

There are also the Upakathas, or minor stories. For instance, about the creation of Bhu-loka, earth. Asuras had pressed down earth into the water after pralaya. From

Brahma's nose emerges a wild boar, Vishnu in his Varaha avatar, which dives into the ocean and brings the earth up. And then plants begin to grow on earth, and creation follows. Another story says the universe was formed out of the Amrita manthan, churning for Amrita. Vishnu brings the Mandar Parvat to churn the Kshir Sagar. He takes his Kurma avatar, the form of a turtle, and supports the mountain on his back. From this manthan, srishti is created. These are three stories where Vishnu is the sleeping Narayana, Varaha or Kurma.

Now, is srishti about prakriti, nature, or sanskriti, culture? The story is that Vishnu had taken the form of a small fish, which Manu saved from the big fish and thus sanskriti came into being. In another story, Vishnu as Hayagriva (horse-headed Vishnu) saves the Vedas from the waters of the pralaya and then srishti is formed. Another story says that before pralaya, a fish goes up to Manu and asks him to carry all living beings, the seeds of plants, and the Vedas in a boat. This is similar to the story of Noah's ark. The fish protects this boat from the waters of the pralaya after which Manu creates the world. The roots of all these stories are there in the different Vedic texts.

What does the Shakta tradition say?

In the Shakta and Tantra traditions, there are many stories, but mainly folklore. The common belief is that when Shiva was meditating, doing tapasya, there was pralaya. Here, pralaya means lifelessness, when everything was frozen and barren. Devi, in the form of Parvati, emerges from the mountain, and seduces him and marries him. The tap, heat or energy, inside him is then released and the snow starts melting. Rivers are formed, the earth becomes fertile, plants and other creatures come alive. So, in the Tantra tradition, purusha, that is, atma, is stirred by Devi and creation happens because of her. Devi is required to awaken the power that is in Shiva.

In folklore, there is a very interesting story, according to which, there were no devas, and the first being was a woman, Adimayashakti. She, in the form of a bird, laid three eggs from which emerged Brahma, Vishnu and Shiva. Adimayashakti asks Brahma to marry her. He says, 'I can't, you are my mother.' She gets angry and curses that he shall never be worshipped. She then asks Vishnu, but he is too shy, so she goes to Shiva. Shiva says, 'I will, only if you give me your third eye.' When he gets the third eye, fire spouts forth from it and reduces her to ashes. The three gods are saddened by the loss of their mother. They wonder what to do, and then, from her ashes, they begin creating devis, perhaps through tap, etc. First emerges Saraswati, who becomes Brahma's wife; then Lakshmi who marries Vishnu; then Parvati who goes to Shiva. From the remaining ashes gramadevis, village goddesses, are created. These are all part of the folk tradition and can't be found in the Puranas. Here, the role of stree, woman, is highlighted.

In Tantra, stree tatva, female essence, comes first, while in the Vedas, purusha tatva, male essence, comes first. Or, it is said that both came together but one was awakened first. In the Vaishnava tradition, they say the world exists but is not experienced until Vishnu awakens. In the Shaiva tradition, the universe cannot begin until Ardhanareshwara splits. In the Shakta tradition, the universe doesn't come into being until Shakti awakens Shiva. It is clearly a complicated process, and perhaps that first hymn of the Vedas reflects it the best—who really knows how creation started!

So there is no 'correct' story?

Even scientists cannot say what the correct story is. Some say it was the Big Bang, others say there was a bang before that. Basically, the question about creation presumes that there was something or nothing before creation. In Hinduism the concept is that the universe is eternal; it is anadi, that is, there is no beginning, and anant, it has no end. There will be a story both before the beginning and after the end, so there can be no single moment of creation.

The question to ask here is whose creation are we speaking about—prakriti, sanskriti, mahabhutas (the elements), vanaspati (plant life) or jeev–jantu (creatures, including human beings). Or is it about mann, the mind—the awakening of the ability to know the world? Just as the question about who created an individual's private experience of the world? We can only create our own worlds, not someone else's—we are all Brahma and create a Brahmanda of our own. It is our unique egg. We create it and then get trapped in it—we're both the hen and the chicken inside the egg. This is the philosophical question. What is creation—the objective world or the subjective world? One cannot exist without the other. So, Hinduism is not interested so much in the mystery of physical creation as much as the larger philosophical approach.

The Bible says the world was created in six days after which came Adam and Eve. Is it the same in our mythology?

Christianity has a linear story. It's one God, one book, one theory that the world was created in seven days, and one way of living is prescribed, known as the Ten Commandments. There was one moment of beginning and there will be one of ending: the apocalypse.

In Hinduism, Buddhism, Jainism, we talk of not *one*, but *multiple*—there are many srishtis, many worlds, many gods. Similarly, there are many beginnings and many ends. Our Manu is equal to Adam. But Manu has a father, Surya, the sun god, whose father is Brahma, from whom came the Sanat-Kumars, the Prajapatis, and so on. There are all kinds of stories, never just one—that is the speciality of Hinduism. You can take your pick, depending on what you prefer—Devi, the sleeping Narayana, the meditating Shiva, the volatile Brahma, or the abstract concepts in the Vedas and Upanishads. It is said that one is born as a human being after 84 lakh yonis, births. Ponder over this idea—it illustrates that we believe in the concept of infinity, not one. Maybe that's why we believe in plurality. Just as there are a variety of flowers, fruit, men, women, so are there countless gods and goddesses, and also stories of creation.

20

Directions

What is Vastu-shastra?

Vastu-shastra is an Indian knowledge system, which believes that if you design a house in a certain way—what is known as architecture or interior decoration—positive energy, peace and prosperity can flow through the house. We live in space, vastu, and time, kaal. Jyotish-shastra or astrology deals with time and Vastu-shastra or geomancy deals with space. Instead of managing oneself, one can successfully manage these external factors.

How is Vastu-shastra related to the Vedas?

In both the Vedas and Vastu-shastra, digga or directions have been given a lot of importance. There are other similarities as well. In Vedic yagnas, smaller fires burn in the west, south and east. The south symbolizes the Pitr or dead ancestors, the east, the gods, and the west, all life. In Vastu, west is for Varuna, god of the sea, and all life comes from water; east is

for Indra, king of the gods; and the south is for Yama, god
of death.

Is Vastu-shastra associated with the Puranas as well?

All directions have their protectors, diggapalas, whose
description is there in the Puranas. There are eight directions—
four cardinal (north, south, east, west) and four ordinal (north-
east, north-west, south-east, south-west)—and two more, above
and below. So there are ten diggapalas. In temples, you'll find
idols of the diggapalas. In the north is Kubera, king of yakshas;
in the south is Yama; in the east is Indra; in the west is Varuna;
in the north-east is Ishan, considered Shiva or the moon; in the
south-west is Nirrti, goddess of death; in the south-east is Agni;
in the north-west is Vayu. All eight idols have a male and a
female elephant on either side, that hold up the sky. Above or at
the top is where Brahma sits and the base is where Vishnu sits.
Some versions say Vishnu sits on Shesh Naga at the base, and
we are inside Vishnu. Vastu Purusha, the human organism or
space in which we exist, is Vishnu's roop. Vishnu's head is in the
north-east and his feet are in the south-west. So space is almost
considered as a human being or a divine being.

What role do the ten diggapalas play in our daily life?

The ten diggapalas indicate a balancing of space, or symmetry.
Kubera, associated with growth, is in the north while Yama,
god of death, is in the south. So, there is a simultaneous
upward and downward movement. Similarly, in the west is
Varuna, associated with salt water, while Indra in the east is
associated with rain water, which is fresh. The way a tent is

propped up by poles and strings in opposite directions, and the way our bodies need to be balanced at all times, the same way balance is important for space.

It appears that the north-east is particularly important; most mandirs inside houses are kept in that direction. Why so?

The north is identified by the Pole Star, a symbol of permanence. Shiva resides on Kailasa in the north. The sun rises in the east so it's a symbol of growth. So the north-east is a combination of permanence and growth—or permanent growth! We want everything! It's primarily associated with good fortune.

There is the well-known story about how the Pole Star came to be. Dhruv is a young prince desiring to win his father's attention and love. His stepmother ensures that it is her son, Uttam, who gets to spend time with her husband, not Dhruv. Young Dhruv goes into the forest and begins to do tapasya. After a long time, Vishnu appears before him; on hearing his desire, he sits him on his own lap and assures him an immoveable place in the sky—as the Dhruv Tara, Pole Star. This story is a metaphor for the permanent love of a devotee for his god, which is reciprocated.

The north is associated with the atma, soul. In order to give the idea of permanence a concrete image, the Dhruv Tara, has been associated with it, as has Shiva who sits in the north on Kailasa, where Meru is also located. He sits under the Dhruv Tara on an unmoving mountain and faces south. In a south Indian temple, there's a famous Shiva idol called Dakshina-murti, that which faces south, imparting the knowledge of the Vedas. It sits under a banyan tree, which too signifies permanence. All these symbols come together to say that the knowledge of the Vedas is eternal, anant, and seamless, akhandit.

Contrary to that, the south has Yama, and the Vaitarni river that separates Bhu-loka and Pitr-loka. Upon death, a body is laid with the head towards the south and legs towards the north so that the head is facing Shiva. During cremation, when the skull is broken, the atma will travel (presumably from the head) towards Pitr-loka in the south. This concept is very important in Hindu rituals, in temples and in the shastras.

How are temples associated with Vastu-shastra?

Typically, all temples are oriented towards the east so that the first rays of the rising sun can fall on the god's idol. The deity faces east and devotees face west; so the sun's rays fall on the god and be reflected on the devotee. Temples are usually imagined as a woman's body, sitting with her knees bent. The place where the idol of god is placed is, in fact, known as the garbha griha, womb. For instance, the temple of Jagannath Puri can be described as a human body, with a head, hands, feet, and so on.

Is there a temple in which the idol is not oriented towards the east?

There are many such temples, because gods change direction depending on the story. For instance, the Mahalakshmi temple in Kolhapur faces west because Lakshmi was born to Varuna.

In another story, Vibhishana, Ravana's younger brother, comes to attend Rama's coronation ceremony. He's considered a great devotee of Vishnu. While departing, he asks Rama to give him his idol to remember him by. Rama gives him an idol of a sleeping Vishnu, Narayana Murti. It is so heavy that Vibhishana puts it down on his way back, at Srirangam, Tamil Nadu, and is unable to carry it to Lanka. The temple there has this idol facing south.

Is there any such story in the Mahabharata?

While the important directions in the Ramayana are primarily north and south, in the Mahabharata all directions come into play. However, Krishna travels from Mathura in the east to Dwarka in the west. Dwarka is an island so there's an elaborate description of the sea.

In ancient India, there were two highways—Uttara-patha, the northern path, and Dakshina-patha, the southern path. Actually, though, the northern highway is going from west to east and the southern from north to south. We can speculate that Dakshina-patha is probably connected with the Ramayana and Uttara-patha with the Mahabharata.

People tend to think that south in the epic implies the south of India, and that it's a problematic zone. We should never take mythological tales literally; they are meant to be symbolic and are attempts to illuminate the human condition. Metaphorically, north represents your head, brain, mind, and the south, your base instincts, your Muladhara chakra where your toxins and negative energies prevail. You must always travel northwards, like the lotus that blooms towards the north. Psychologically, it is up and down, which can also be denoted as north and south.

It is unfortunate that the British theory that these texts actually imply that devas reside in the north and rakshasas or asuras in the south is still popular. This has made it a political matter, because of which the spiritual essence of these texts gets lost. I personally feel that the Puranas and Vastu-shastra are discussing spiritual matters.

21

Marriage

Most of our gods and goddesses are married and have families. Why is that?

The two most important concepts in Hindu philosophy are prakriti or nature—which is sagun, and denotes the physical world—and purusha or atma, soul—which is nirgun, and denotes the spiritual world. You shouldn't take purusha literally to mean man; it is a metaphor. Vivaah, marriage, is the union of the body and the soul. So when it is said in temples that there is a wedding of Shiva, Vishnu or Rama, this is what is implied.

We know Rama has one wife, Sita. Later, when Vishnu becomes Krishna, he has eight wives. How many wives does Vishnu have?

In the animal kingdom, there are no marriages. Marriages are a concept of sanskriti, culture. Some animals like the rajhans and cheel have only one mate for their entire life, while elephants, lions, tigers, do not. Bees, for instance, have a queen bee that controls everything. So, in prakriti, there are different kinds of systems for different species. Similarly, in the Puranas, it is said that in different kaals, yugas, samajs (times, eras and societies), there are different vyavasthas (systems). In the Ramayana, Rama is ekampatnivrata (a monogamist) but not Dashratha, his father, who had three wives (Kaikeyi, Sumitra and Kaushalya). Krishna in the Bhagavata Purana is said to be polygamous and has eight wives; Draupadi in the Mahabharata has five husbands, that is, she practises polyandry. There is no right or wrong, only different systems that are followed depending on the social set-up. There is no one ideal or perfect system. In fact, Rama's state of monogamy is rare.

We've heard a lot about Shiva's wedding, but hardly anything about Vishnu's. Tell us about it.

Usually, it is slipped in somewhere between other stories, and Vishnu is always assumed to be married—that's the reason his story isn't well known. There are two different versions. In south India, alongside Vishnu's idols are the idols of his two wives, Shridevi, aishwarya or wealth, and Bhudevi, who is earth. Both are roops of Lakshmi. In north India, however, it's just Lakshmi.

When Hiranyaksha abducts Bhudevi and hides her under the ocean, Vishnu, in the form of Varaha, rescues her. She tells him she considers him her husband, so his name becomes Bhupati. From the Amrita manthan emerges Shridevi. Both the devas and the asuras fight over her, but she says she'll choose her own husband, and chooses Vishnu. So he becomes Shrinivas or Shripati. Both are typical south

Indian names. In the north, he is Lakshmi Vallabha, the beloved of Lakshmi.

There are few gods who are brahmacharis, bachelors—why?

There are two schools of thought: one that says in order to do good by society, you should be married, and the other that says brahmacharya, celibacy, brings you power, ojas or tap. Hanuman, a brahmachari, is called vajra angi, Bajrang, that is, one with the body of steel. Certain manifestations, or roops, of gods are unmarried, like Shiva's Bhairava roop, Murugan's Dandapani roop, etc. Ganapati is sometimes depicted as married (to Riddhi and Siddhi) and sometimes as a bachelor. It depends on which school of thought you prescribe to. There's a perennial debate in India about whether Shiva is unmarried, as he's a vairagi, or married since he has two children (Kartikeya and Ganesha). But even Kartikeya's birth is always shown to be different from a natural birth. A belief that is very popular in India is that once you marry and have children, you lose some of your power. It cannot be proved scientifically, but in Tantra this is of utmost importance.

Devis are called kumaris. Are they brahmachari?

There is a contradiction because Devi is kumari (from kunwari, unmarried) as well as a mata, mother. It should perhaps be seen as a metaphor. A field is a fertile virgin, kumari, before it is ploughed. After the rains, when it produces the crop, it is called mata. So Devi is known as kumari mata. As kumari she wears red and as mata, green.

Devi in her vira, warrior, heroic, or ugra, terrifying, roop is considered unmarried. There is no male aspect to her; she's completely female. There is a very interesting story in the south. The southern tip of India is called Kanyakumari, the kanya, woman, who is not married. She is a gramadevi, a village deity, who wanted to marry Shiva. The devas did not want her to do so because it would reduce her power. So they go to stop her. They tell her only she can kill Bana-asura whose powers are constantly increasing. She says she knows only a kumari can kill him; and if not she, someone else will. She insists on being married. The devas enlist the help of Narada who says he'll exploit Shiva's naivety. He waylays Shiva, and tells him that the midnight muhurat, auspicious time, designated for the wedding is past and it is almost dawn. Shiva believes him and turns back towards Kailasa. Devi waits interminably and weeps in despair. All her make-up flows down with her tears. That's why they say the waters at the Triveni Sangam at Kanyakumari have various colours. After this sad turn of events, she assumes the ugra roop and kills Bana.

Most of our gods are polygamous but our society is not . . .

Society keeps changing. Even until 100 years ago, polygamy was commonly practised in India—men were allowed to have many wives. Of course, a woman was never allowed more than one husband. However, in times before that, women had greater freedom. There is a dialogue in the Mahabharata between Pandu and Kunti which suggests that men and women were free to choose their mates. There were no concepts of fidelity and marriage rituals.

There is a story about how that changed. A young boy, Shwetaketu, tells his father Uddalaka, 'I don't like seeing my mother with other men,' but he is told that their sabhyata, culture, is like that. His mother is free to do what she wants. Shwetaketu says, 'Then how do I know you are my father?' Uddalaka says a man becomes a father by love, not seed. It's a sophisticated thought, and this story is not often told. From then on, Shwetaketu made a rule that a wife would have to be faithful to her husband, and she would not have the freedom to choose a man. At one time, there used to be a swayamvara where a woman chose her own husband. Gradually, that practice went away as patriarchy became more and more entrenched. Men could keep many wives, but women couldn't do the same. Some say society improved because of it, some say it deteriorated. In my personal opinion, though, people should be allowed freedom.

In folklore and the Puranas, there are many romantic stories behind weddings of gods and goddesses. What is the mystery behind these stories?

There are different types of vivaah described in the texts. One is asura vivaah, where the bride is bought. Another is deva vivaah, in which a father donates his daughter in recognition of good work done by the man. In rishi vivaah, a rishi needs a wife to perform yagna so a king or father will give him his daughter. Pishacha vivaah is one that's done by force. In Brahma vivaah, a groom seeks permission from a father to marry his daughter. The most popular one in stories is gandharva vivaah, or love marriage. Now, each grama (village) has gramadevis. You will see that gods usually have two wives—loka patni (earthly wife, or the gramadevi) and aloka patni (who's related to the gods).

Or a bhoga patni (for everyday needs) and a moksha patni (associated with spirituality). All this is at the conceptual level, and is presented through shringara rasa, romantic form, in stories.

Once, Murugan falls in love with a tribal princess called Valli. He asks for Ganesha's help, telling him to become an elephant to scare her, so that he can hold her in his arms and drive the elephant away. Here, God has become humanlike. Perhaps romance assumed importance because at one time there were the rishis doing yagnas on the one hand, which no one understood, and on the other, sanyasis and vairagis spoke of renunciation. They took no interest in women, in family life, shaved off their heads and declared the world to be merely maya, an illusion. Common people began to wonder whether there was any relationship at all between God and the enjoyment of life. That's where these romantic stories came in, to convey that gods too like to be in love and enjoy life; Vishnu, Shiva, Krishna are taking part in material existence (samsaric jeevan). These stories bring in the higher concepts of yoga, of the union of prakriti and purusha, etc., in a fun way, but in a celebratory idiom (utsav, shringara, vivaah).

Can human beings also marry gods?

In our country, anything can happen! In Puranic stories, many humans do marry gods. In ancient times, there used to be ganikas, or courtesans, who were free. In the medieval age, ganikas married gods, and came to be called devadasis, god's maids. These women too were free. A devadasi was sada suhagan—a woman whose husband, god, was always alive—and she could choose her lovers. Later, this system became exploitative and was abolished. Bhakts, devotees, also sometimes marry gods. For instance, Mirabai declared Krishna to be her husband. Even male devotees can declare themselves god's dasi, or wife.

22

Shape-shifting

In Puranic stories, gods change forms, take on different roops. Elaborate on this.

What should be God's roop? God is anant and akhandit, timeless and indivisible, and all forms are included in him—like the Vishwa-rupa—so what is his form? Is God a he or a she? Is he old or young? Some people say he has form (sagun), some say he doesn't (nirgun). Puranic stories discuss this a lot, and so, he is given various forms—brahmachari, purusha, devi, deva, plant, animal, and so on.

A thousand years ago, in ancient Hinduism, in loka dharma, folk religion, people worshipped stones and trees as gods. They believed rocks housed yakshas, water contained apsaras, and plants housed gandharvas. In the Bhagavata Purana, there's a story where Krishna uproots a tree and breaks it into two from which two gandharvas emerge. In animal form, cows are worshipped as mother, go-mata. Some take it literally, but it can also be seen symbolically. Prakriti, nature, is believed to be a cow, as it is her yield from which we get sustenance, the 'milk' of life.

Why are two beings merged to create one?

The idea is to stretch the imagination as far as possible. There is Ganesha, a man's body with an elephant's head; Hayagriva, who is Vishnu's roop with a horse's head; Narasimha who is half-human, half-lion, and so on. In that famous story, the asura Hiranyakashipu obtains a vardaan, that he can only be killed by a creature that is neither man nor animal, thus creating a division. Vishnu creates the Narasimha form to show that there is no division in the world of God.

This is a recurrent theme in other stories as well. In Odisha, there's a Sarala Das Mahabharata which has a story of Nabagunjara, in which Krishna takes the form of nine animals and goes to Arjuna. The Pandava is frightened by the creature—a combination of cock, peacock, bull, tiger, elephant, snake. It is beyond his imagination, and that's the idea—what may be called 'monster' is a form of God in Puranic stories. In the Shaiva tradition, Shiva takes the form of a Sharabha, a lion with eight legs. The word unnatural has a negative connotation, but to explain spiritual concepts gods have to take on 'unnatural' forms; here unnatural becomes positive. So, Lakshmi has four arms, Vishnu has ten heads, Hanuman has five or ten heads, etc. All kinds of beings—plants and trees, animals, asura, deva, gandharva—can be seen in Krishna's Vishwarupa in the Gita.

Can women take on male forms and vice versa?

Yes, there are no such permanent divisions in the stories. Vishnu takes the form of an apsara, Mohini, where moh means to attract. Mohini is able to attract the asuras as well as Shiva. In Yog Vasishtha, a king believes women are ignorant, while his queen is very knowledgeable. She sometimes takes the form of a man, sometimes woman, to show him that knowledge and gender are not related. It is to make us look beyond external features that God breaks the idea of such divisions.

Is that what is called maya?

In the Vedas, the word maya has many meanings. Sometimes, it means just power or magical power, as in the word mayajaal, web of maya. Vishnu is known as Mayavi, but there are mayavi asuras too. It has to do with intent. When you acquire magical powers, siddha, by doing intense meditation, you can change your form. God is already a siddha, but humans can achieve it too. But why you change form, that is important. If it's only for selfish reasons, then it becomes jaadu-tona, black magic, and is manipulative.

In a story, Indra takes the form of Rishi Gautama so that he can sleep with the rishi's wife, Ahalya. He breaks her wifely fidelity. Enraged, Gautama curses Indra and causes his body to be covered in bleeding sore and blisters all over. Asuras can also change their form. Mahisha-asura can take the form of a buffalo, elephant, lion, even human. Once, Adi-asura takes Shiva's form to possess Parvati, but she recognizes him with her divya drishti, divine vision.

In one story, Shankhachuda, an asura, is blessed with invincibility as long as his wife Vrinda remains pativrata, loyal to her husband. Vishnu takes the form of the asura and goes to her; the moment she thinks he is her husband, she loses her purity and Shankhachuda is killed in battle. When he tells her that she betrayed him, Vrinda finds out about Vishnu's treachery. Out of dismay, she becomes a tulsi plant. Vishnu feels sorry, and says that his puja will remain incomplete until a tulsi leaf is offered, thus acknowledging a loyal wife. This is prevalent only in some regions in India, although it's there in the Puranas.

All these stories complicate the matter of shape-shifting; when it is right and when not. For instance, when Parvati is doing tap, Shiva tests her by taking various forms—a handsome man, then an old man—asking her why she is marrying Shiva, a vairagi whose body is smeared with ash. Then there are loka kathas, folk tales, about this. Santoshima's vrata kathas, which are told during fasting, are famous. In one, she takes the form of an old woman and sits on the side of the road as a beggar to test her devotees, to see whether they respect her in this form or not. So, God can appear in any form any time.

There is a face and a mask, and Ravana wants to wear Rama's mask. But it's not easy to take on a god's mask or outer form, because when you do, you have to acquire the god's qualities as well. It transforms you from within. That's what Ravana experiences when he loses his ego and is unable to kill his servant.

In another such story, a man declares he has become Krishna by wearing a crown and sticking a peacock feather in it. Krishna says, 'Sure, you are Krishna now. Here, take this Sudarshan chakra.' And the man is crushed under its weight.

Is there a story where Shiva changes his form?

All gods do that and there are many such stories about Shiva. In a story from south India, there is an old woman, a Shiva bhakt, who wants to visit her pregnant daughter who is in labour. A sudden flood prevents her and she prays to Shiva. Shiva takes an old woman's form and goes as a midwife to the daughter and delivers the baby.

There is a story from Mathura, about Krishna performing the raas-leela in Vrindavana. In the raas-leela, there's always one man—Krishna, the purnapurusha, complete man—while all the others are gopikas, milkmaids, his companions. Other gods want to watch this famous leela, but are not allowed. So they go to Yamuna who tells them to take a dip in her waters after which she gives them a female form. Thus, Narada, Arjuna, and even Shiva participate in this leela. Once, Radha is upset when she sees Krishna dancing with another woman. Krishna tells her that this is his guru. Krishna is a natwar, expert in dance, and his guru is Nataraja, the god of dance, another name for Shiva. And since she has placed restrictions on men coming to the Vrindavana forest, Shiva had to take a female form. This interchanging of male and female forms is common. But it's important to focus on the underlying concept or theme.

23

Avatars of Vishnu

What does avatar mean?

The word avatar comes from avataran, coming down from above. Above is Vaikuntha, the heavenly abode where there is no death. When gods take an avatar, they become mortal. They will be born of the womb, grow old and experience death. From being infinite, they become finite, immortal to mortal. They take an avatar to do uddhar, improve the lot of mankind.

How many avatars does Vishnu have?

Commonly, it is believed that he has ten avatars, but that idea emerged only 1000 years ago, with Jayadev's *Gita Govinda*. If you go back to the Puranas, there is no fixed number; there could be ten, twenty, or more than thirty avatars. Among the commonly known ten, Mohini isn't included, but the Bhagavata Purana talks of many kinds of avatars, including Mohini (a female form), a rajhans (swan), a rishi (Vyas). The lists of Vishnu's avatars in the Bhagavata

Purana and the Vishnu Purana vary; there's no standard set of his avatars.

So which are the ten popularly known avatars?

These are Matsya (fish), Kurma (turtle), Varaha (wild boar), Narasimha (half-human, half-lion), Vamana (dwarf then giant), Parashurama, Rama, Krishna, Buddha and Kalki. But this list too isn't fixed. Jayadev's *Gita Govinda*, from where the concept of the dashavatar has taken root, does not include Krishna in the list. Instead, Balarama is the eighth avatar, while Buddha is the ninth. Buddha is described for the first time here. Elsewhere, the eighth and ninth avatars are Krishna and Balarama. Although scholars dispute over the more 'accurate' list, there's no right or wrong list; there's only a popular list.

Is Buddha really an avatar of Vishnu?

This is a controversial question! There was a time in ancient India when there was a lot of philosophical dispute between Hinduism and Buddhism, when both competed for supremacy. They must've each marketed themselves too. So, the Hindus simply included Buddha as an avatar, to say that by worshipping Buddha you are ultimately worshipping Vishnu. Buddhists, of course, did not accept this, and still don't.

It is said that Buddha took the form of a Bodhisattva on earth to uplift mankind, like Vishnu did . . .

When Buddhism was established 2500 years ago, Buddha said desire was the cause of pain and suffering, which can end by renouncing the world and achieving nirvana. Gradually, people began to feel that was not a feasible way to live. This virakti, disgust, with the world was too extreme. They wondered if there wasn't a middle path. This form of Buddhism was also too masculine—his idols were purely masculine; there was no female energy there. So, Buddhism started changing.

The old practice, Theravada, changed to Mahayana around 2000 years ago. This has the Bodhisattva concept. Here, Buddha says he will not take nirvana; instead, he will stay on earth to uplift society. This is also the time when Jataka tales begin to be told about Buddha's earlier lives, where he did many good deeds as Bodhisattva and accumulated karma to eventually be born as Buddha. This is the same period when Hinduism is shifting from Vedic to Puranic. From the yagna tradition to that of telling stories, kathas, a time when stories of Vishnu, Shiva, Devi emerge. Here, the avatar concept takes root; God is eternal and infinite, but he takes birth on earth to help human beings. Bodhisattva is popular even today in China, Japan and South East Asia. Here, Bodhisattva has multiple arms and heads. Vishnu too has four arms, chaturbhuj, and many heads, but when he takes a human avatar, he has only two arms and a single head.

It is said in the Puranas that at the end of the Kali Yuga, Vishnu's avatar Kalki will appear. Has he appeared already or is he going to appear? What are your thoughts on this?

In the Puranas, the story of Kalki comes at a time when tribes from the north-west—the Huns, Gujjars, Yavanas—were coming into the country from what we know as Afghanistan, Uzbekistan, Central Asia today. There were many raids since

India was prosperous and wealthy. So, the story of Kalki was perhaps created to imagine a saviour riding on horseback—somewhat like the raiders—who would save us. At this time, we were also interacting and trading with Christians and Jews who believe in the concept of a messiah who will demolish the old order and bring in a new world. Perhaps the concept of Kalki was inspired by this. That when immorality and corruption become rampant, Vishnu will take the form of a warrior and destroy everything, and create the world anew. All traditions and sanskritis, cultures, have the concept of a messiah because most times we feel we are living in terrible times and must be saved.

What learning do we get from Vishnu's avatars?

In our ancient texts, the recurring question is, do you want to participate in the world or not? Shiva doesn't wish to be part of the world at all, so he has no avatars. But Vishnu the preserver, through his avatars, takes on the task of showing how one can practise spirituality while being part of the world. Take his Matsya avatar. When a bigger fish eats a smaller fish, it is natural, and is called matsya nyaya, the law of the fish. Once, a small fish—Vishnu in his Matsya avatar—begs Manu to save him from a big fish. When Manu saves the small fish, it marks the beginning of culture, sanskriti, which is based on different rules. Vishnu's Kurma avatar is about balance. In Amrita manthan, you need a support, a pivot on which the churning can be done. This support is provided by Vishnu, as Kurma, a turtle. Similarly, to live your life, you need mental stability. Varaha shows the value of force; Narasimha shows the value of wit, cleverness, and so on. Each of his avatars offers a piece of wisdom.

The concept of avatar is associated with establishing dharma, moral order. There is a famous shloka in the Bhagavad Gita where Vishnu says that whenever there is adharma, immorality, on earth, 'I will come down to re-establish dharma.' This is only associated with the Vaishnava tradition, not Shakta or Shaiva. Although local texts do talk of Shiva's avatars, for instance, Hanuman is said to be his avatar or ansh. In the Shakta tradition too, Mahavidya, Matrika, Yogini are all considered Devi's avatars.

It is believed that Vishnu always comes to earth when Devi is suffering. When Renuka is troubled, Vishnu takes the form of Parashurama, her son. He is Rama for Sita. In the Bhagavata Purana, there is a story in which Bhudevi, the earth goddess, appears before Vishnu in the form of a cow, and describes the corruption and selfishness that has taken root among human beings. She weeps, saying she feels terribly exploited and disrespected. Vishnu promises her that he will come to earth as a cowherd (Krishna) to protect her. The other belief is that every time Vishnu takes an avatar, Devi too is born. The relationship between the Shaiva and Shakta traditions is always one of husband and wife, but the one between Shakta and Vaishnava is variable. Devi can be a mother, wife, friend, sister. Draupadi is believed to be a form of Devi, especially in the south; and it is even said that Yogamaya is Vishnu's sister. So, Vishnu comes in the form that Devi requires.

Two Vishnu avatars—Rama and Parashurama—exist at the same time. How is that possible?

Firstly, you should never apply logic to mythological stories—they aren't supposed to make logical sense! And a simple explanation is that since Vishnu is God he can choose to do whatever he wants—even exist as two avatars at once!

Jokes apart, perhaps when the stories were written, there was no concept of avatars. The concept was later added on to these stories; some said Rama, others said Parashurama, and still others said both were avatars of Vishnu. These stories are not fixed; they evolved from many different texts, periods and regions, and eventually came to be tied up together. Parashurama is born to kill Kiratavirya-arjuna, an adharmi, corrupt, king. He kills many such kings violently with his axe; apparently, he kills all Kshatriyas. Finally, the other gods plead with him to stop, saying the world needs warriors and kings too. He says he'll stop the day he meets a good Kshatriya. When he meets Rama, he's convinced of Rama's virtue, and stops. It's as though his role ends and Rama's begins.

Is there a connection between Vishnu's avatars and Charles Darwin's theory of evolution?

Darwin challenged the Christian belief that the world was created by God in seven days. According to his theory, first there were micro-organisms, then aquatic animals, then four-legged animals, then humans; that is, we came to be through an evolutionary process. When this knowledge reached India, it was correlated to Vishnu's avatars: first fish, then turtle, then boar, then Narasimha (evolving between animal and human), then Vamana (dwarf human), then Parashurama (fully grown human). As you see, the thought was there, but whether or not it was the same as Darwin's concept is a moot question.

In Vishnu's avatars, the first four are animals. Once human beings come, Vamana onwards, the varna, or caste, system comes in. Vamana and Parashurama are Brahmins;

Rama is a Kshatriya; Krishna is of indeterminate varna since he is a warrior, but also a cowherd and a sarathi; and Buddha has rejected the caste system. Kalki is said to come from outside, riding a horse, and so no caste can be ascribed to him, although some claim he is a Brahmin. It is an interesting transition from animal to human and then to the caste system, although what exactly it means is disputed among scholars.

24

Stars and Planets

Why do the Vedas give so much importance to stars and planets?

In the Vedas, three mandalas are given a lot of importance. Mandala means circle—a combination of anda, egg, and mann, mind. Bhu-mandala is the earth, above that is Prabha-mandala, the sky, where it is believed the gods reside, and there is Pitr-loka, the land of dead ancestors. You can look at Prabha-mandala and predict when summer, winter, monsoons will arrive; it works like a clock. When the grahas (planets), moon, stars, move from one place to another, you can say how the temperature will change, etc. There seems to be a system, a rhythm to the workings of the world. Because of this it was believed that the gods lived there, managing the clock of the seasons.

Vedic rituals are mostly oriented towards the sky; which is the reason agni is worshipped, since it goes upwards. It is believed that if you put ghee in fire, it'll reach the gods, Indra, Surya, Chandra or Som. Trees are also known as som as they grow towards the sky, Prabha-mandala. All Vedic shlokas are addressed to the sky. In the Puranas, however, the earth is also given value. Gramadevis (village goddesses) are on earth. Sky is the male principle and earth, the female principle. Above is Shiva and below is Shakti.

What is a nakshatra? Is it not the same as a rashi?

Prabha-mandala, the sky, is full of stars that are natural. But ancient civilizations—Babylon, China, India—clustered them together to form different constellations and gave them different shapes and names. It was a way of dividing the sky. One such cluster of twelve divisions is the zodiac, or rashi, comprising constellations like Capricorn, Aries, and so on. In India, we also have twenty-seven divisions, called nakshatras, like Rohini, Vishakha, Phalguni. These are actually twenty-six, because one of them, Abhijeet, is invisible. So the sky is divided into twelve rashis and twenty-seven nakshatras.

Are all nakshatras female?

Nakshatras are all considered Daksha Prajapati's daughters. Daksha marries twenty-seven of his daughters to Chandra, the moon god, who prefers Rohini above his other wives. Once, Daksha and Chandra have an argument over the moon's favouritism and lack of responsibility towards his other wives. Chandra is about to leave the king's palace in a huff, abandoning his other wives in their father's home. Angered, the king curses him that just as he's abandoned his daughters, his body, his light, his shape will abandon him and he will be completely hidden. Chandra goes to Shiva for help. He's learnt his lesson. Shiva offers a compromise where Chandra

will regain his shape slowly before he begins to lose it again—
and thus the cycle will continue. Thus, it is said, the moon
goes to each one of the nakshatras (Chandra's wives) by turn
every day. He's with Rohini on the night of the full moon, and
starts waning gradually, until on the night of the new moon he
is with Abhijeet.

What are grahas?

Grahas are celestial bodies, not only planets, so the sun too is
a graha. Since they are moving, they are masculine, while the
steady stars are feminine.

Are there any stories about them? Tell us about the sun.

The sun is associated with romance. The flower known as
raat ki rani, or queen of the night, is said to have been in
love with the sun, but he was not interested. She becomes
so sad that she decides to bloom only when he's not in the
sky. The sunflower, on the other hand, keeps looking at him,
even though he ignores her and just charts his course across
the sky.

**So, both the sun and moon are basically heartbreakers! Tell
us about Mangal and Budh.**

Mangal rashi is associated with war, violence and aggression,
and with Kartikeya, the god of war. In some stories, he is
related with the ugra roop of Ganesha. The word Mangal
refers to the planet Mars, and it also means shubh, auspicious,
from mangalya. It's red colour connects it with Devi, whose
son is known as Mangal.

Budh graha is associated with communication, intelligence, articulation, and with the planet Mercury. It is interesting that in idols and paintings, sometimes he is depicted as a woman even though grahas are usually masculine. This is because Budh is a hermaphrodite, as a result of being cursed by his father.

Budh's consort is Ila. This is an interesting story. A Chandravanashi king, Ila, goes to a jungle where Shiva and Shakti are having sex. There is a spell on the jungle that turns anyone who enters into a woman; the king too falls victim to it. Distraught, he goes to Shiva who modifies the curse, so that he becomes a man during the Shukla Pakshya (period of waxing moon) and a woman during the Krishna Pakshya (period of waning moon). So, Ila, half-man, half-woman, and Budh unite and become the progenitors of the Chandravanash. What is interesting to note here is that the description of persons we know today as queer or homosexual existed in Puranic tales, which some people deny.

Do you have a story about Guru?

Brihaspati, Jupiter, is called Guru because he is the guru of all the gods. Thursday is named after him—Brihaspativar or Guruvar. Shukra, after whom Shukravar, Friday, is named, is also a guru, but of asuras, and there's always a conflict between the two. It is said that Shukracharya, Venus, has only one eye and is creative. Brihaspati has two eyes and is rational, planned, systematic. In a business team, you will observe that there is one member who is on top of all the financial calculations, and is very mathematical in outlook, while there is one member who follows no rules, works at night instead of during the day, but is highly creative. You need the qualities of both devas and asuras, so that the manthan can be done and butter can emerge from the Kshir Sagar.

What about Shani?

Shanidev or Saturn is one of the sons of Surya, the sun god, and Saturday is named after him: Shanivar. He is a sad, slow god, who can't even walk properly, and so he delays everything. If his influence is in your life, you will get everything but slowly, after a lot of waiting. He is there to teach you patience.

You said that all the nakshatras are feminine; are all the stars feminine as well?

No, not really; for instance, Dhruv Tara is male. The constellation Saptarishi mandala, or the Great Bear, isn't either. There is an interesting story about the Sapta Rishis, or seven rishis. They had married seven daughters of Daksh Prajapati. For a yagna, the seven rishis go towards the agnikund, pit of fire, accompanied by their wives. Agni, the fire god, is attracted by the beauty of the wives and touches all but one of them without their realizing it. He misses Arundhati, Vasishtha's wife, who is at a distance. When the wives go to the rishis, the rishis say, 'You've been touched by another man, and have had an extramarital affair; we will not allow you entry into the yagna space.' The women plead innocence, and eventually leave, offended by the accusation. These six are called the Kritika stars, and form their own constellation. The seventh, Arundhati, stands next to the Saptarishi mandala. In a wedding custom, when a newlywed wife is asked, what kind of wife she wants to be, she must say 'like Arundhati' and point to the star in the sky. If she doesn't know where it is, the husband has to hold her hand and point in that direction. The ritual is romantic because this is the first time the husband and wife touch each other.

Tell us some stories about rashis, the zodiac.

Among the zodiac, Makara, Capricorn, and Karka, Cancer, are the most important. The day of Makara Sankranti is when the sun enters the house of Capricorn. It's the beginning of Uttarayan, that is, the sun starts moving in the northern direction, and the weather becomes warmer, indicating the arrival of spring. When it moves into Karka, Dakshinayan begins; the rising sun moves in the southern direction. Karka is like a crab, it holds you back, so days become shorter, nights longer, temperature cools, rains arrive. It is said that during this time asuras become powerful. Festivals like Dussehra, Diwali, and so on are celebrated at this time in order to awaken the gods and ask them to kill the asuras. The two movements are compared to Amrita manthan: when the devas pull, the days grow longer, when the asuras pull, the days grow shorter. In Prabha-mandala, Amrita manthan is on throughout the year. Half the year, the gods are powerful, and in the other half, the asuras. So we worship Sura and asura both.

Vishnu wears makara earrings, so is he connected with the rashi in some way?

Vishnu is called Makarakundala, he whose earrings are like makara. After Makara Sankranti, spring begins and life blossoms. Vishnu is associated with this positive side of nature, and so with Shukla Pakshya, Uttarayan, etc. He is associated with the sun, and is also known as Aditya. During Makara Sankranti, the sun is worshipped.

Shiva, on the other hand, is associated with the moon. He wears a crescent on his head, and is called Somashekhar. He is associated with the other cycle—Dakshinayan, Krishna Pakshya, and so on. Prabha-mandala and the cycle of seasons are thus divided equally between Vishnu and Shiva.

25

Plants and Gods

Do we worship plants, vanaspati, as gods because we receive food and medicine from them?

Yes, we do. Since the Vedic period, we have been in awe of the fact that every plant or tree has some quality. They provide food, medicine, wood, all the things that sustain life. Our ancestors felt that gods reside in the trees. In the Vedas there's a devi called Aranyani, goddess of the forest, and Shakambari, goddess of vegetation, in the Puranas.

Our sanskriti, culture, has its roots in the jungle, that's where it all began, so trees are given a lot of value. It was believed that if the value of all the trees were to be combined, it would yield Amrita. In Amrita manthan, the mountain that is used to churn has numerous trees growing on it. During the intense churning, they rub against each other and catch fire, such that their juices flow down, adding to the existing Amrita in the Kshir Sagar. From the churning also emerged the Parijat tree, which some believe to be the Kalpavriksh. It is so wonderful that Indra takes it with him to heaven.

Once, Naraka asura attacks Swarga and a battle ensues, in which Krishna supports Indra and defeats the asuras. Krishna's wife Satyabhama had accompanied him to heaven before the battle. She tells Krishna to ask for the Parijat tree in return for his help. Indra does not want to part with the tree. The tree is so important that Indra and Krishna fight over it. When the Parijat finally arrives in Bhu-loka, Krishna asks Satyabhama to show it to the other queens. She becomes possessive, but then she asks Rukmini, one of Krishna's wives, to keep it in her garden, so she doesn't have to work on maintaining it. But she places it in such a way that all the branches bloom in her garden, and she can enjoy the flowers of the night-flowering jasmine. Krishna learns of this deceit, and says that the Parijat tree will only bloom when he is with Rukmini. So every time the tree blooms, Satyabhama's ill-deserved joy is tempered. These are folk tales, to infuse some lightness and mischief into the lives of the gods.

What are the different plants offered to the different gods and goddesses?

In Shiva temples, bel leaf and wild datura flowers are offered. In the Kashi Vishwanath temple, some bhang (marijuana leaf) is offered as well. Hanuman is offered arka flowers (*Calotropis indica*), which are poisonous and purple in colour. Since Hanuman is a brahmachari, he's offered this wild roadside plant that is easily available. Vishnu is offered fragrant flowers and leaves like champa (*Plumeria*), tulsi, lotus. Krishna is vanamali, he who wears a garland of forest flowers. Ganesha is offered durva (blades of grass), betel nut flower, paan and betel nut, and marigolds. Each marigold petal has a seed, which is a symbol of fertility. Garlands of marigold flowers are hung on doorways during pujas, strung along with mango leaves. Mango is offered to Vishnu and Ganesha because they are the gods of householders, but never to Shiva. Devis are not offered anything, but neem leaf, lemon, chillies, tamarind leaf are used in their puja—all the strong flavours.

What is the significance of offering durva to Ganesha?

When you uproot durva or blades of grass, they grow back; grass cannot be completely destroyed. It always grows somewhere or the other. Rishis say it may be because Amrita has touched it. In the Puranas, the Amrita kalash was kept on grass, which makes it holy. It can be seen as a symbol of permanence, and we want prosperity and success to be permanent, so durva is given importance in yagnas and pujas. The priest who conducts the puja wears a grass ring on his finger.

How was vanaspati created in the Brahmanda, the cosmos?

The stories around this are not popularly known. One such is that plants were born out of Brahma's hair. Another story is that when Bhudevi is abducted by Hiranyaksha, Varaha brings her back from under the ocean. In the process, his tusks plunge into the earth, and that's how vanaspati was born. One of my favourite stories about this is from the Ramayana. When Sita disappears into the earth, Rama tries to catch her, but only a few strands of her hair are left behind. These become grass.

What are the different plant metaphors we use to praise the beauty of our gods and goddesses?

In Sanskrit literature, plants and animals, beings of the natural world, are used to create similes, metaphors, adages, etc., to explain things. For instance, Vishnu is called Kamalnayan, one with lotus-like eyes. There's a story from the Krittivasa Ramayana of Bengal. Rama worships Durga and says he'll offer her 108 lotus flowers. She wants to test him so she steals one flower. Seeing there are only 107, he wonders what to do. He remembers that his mother compared his eyes to the lotus and so offers one of his eyes to Durga. There's a similar story in the Puranas where Vishnu does the same for Shiva and thus acquires the Sudarshan chakra. So, eyes have been equated with the lotus.

Apsaras' hands have been compared to latas, graceful creepers. Even in Buddhist viharas, monasteries, you'll find a famous image of latanayika—a beautiful woman, covered in ornaments, holding a tree branch. In popular Hindi films too you'll see the heroine clasping a tree branch and swaying happily. This image is considered to be shubh, auspicious. If a beautiful woman sings and dances in a forest, it is believed to be a very good thing. These days we don't think of women doing that—perhaps we've become backward now! But in the Gupta period, it was said that during spring, only when women made merry, sang and danced around trees, would the trees burst into life, and kadam, ashoka, and other flowers bloom. If a woman is sad, the earth will not flower. So, laughing, rejoicing women were celebrated, and the correlation between women and nature, prakriti, was highlighted in this wonderful way.

Why do women tie a thread around the bargad, banyan, tree, and how is the tree significant?

The banyan, vatvriksha, is very important in India because it provides shade over a wide area. What is interesting, however, is that it's considered shubh as well as ashubh, because nothing grows under a banyan tree due to its large canopy. For example, you respect a sanyasi but keep him out of your house. You allow only a married priest inside the house, and similarly, a banyan tree is kept at a distance from the house. If grown too close, it can break the house.

In villages, the banyan is kept near the cremation ground, where it is believed ghosts live. As Shiva likes and lives with ghosts, the banyan tree is associated with him. But, the banyan leaf is associated with Krishna and Vishnu. It is said that when pralaya, doomsday, will arrive, and everything is being destroyed, a banyan leaf will be floating on the waves of the deluge. On the leaf there will be a baby, a roop of Vishnu, called Vatpatra Sai, child on the banyan leaf.

When Markandeya is shown what pralaya will be like, he is frightened to see all the villages, living beings getting submerged in the flood. Then he has a vision of Vatpatra Sai, a happy baby with butter on his fingers, floating fearlessly on a banyan leaf. So, this is also associated with Krishna.

Bhakti or devotion is explained through the medium of vanaspati. For instance, tulsi is said to be Vrinda devi. We keep a tulsi plant in the house and it needs to be maintained every day; it is always seen as a woman, also considered to be Radha by some. A tulsi leaf is offered to Krishna.

There is an interesting story about the significance of the tulsi. Once, Satyabhama loses Krishna to Narada in a wager, making Krishna Narada's servant. Satyabhama tells Krishna it can be avoided if she gives something heavier than him to Narada. She asks for a balance and asks Krishna to sit on one side and puts all her jewellery and wealth on the other side. However, Krishna's side of the balance remains heavier. Then Rukmini adds just one tulsi leaf to Satyabhama's side and the balance tilts. Krishna tells Satyabhama it's because that one leaf contains all of Rukmini's bhakti, devotion, whereas Satyabhama's wealth contains only her aham, ego.

While flowers, fruit, leaves, etc., are useful as food and medicine, they are also symbols. Here, tulsi is a symbol of bhakti, like the bel leaf for Shiva. In the story, the weight of Rukmini's devotion is greater than Krishna himself, and that is expressed through a lightweight tulsi leaf. So, the story demonstrates the value of metaphors and symbols.

Why do we break coconuts in temples?

The coconut has to be broken in one go, and sometimes, a tikka is applied on it before it is broken. There is a theory that some people like, but others don't. According to this, in earlier times, bali, sacrifice, was offered—either of animals or human beings—during puja. Since we cannot continue with that practice in real terms, because of animal rights or simply because we prefer the path of ahimsa, we can do it symbolically with the coconut. Some say breaking the coconut is a mark of breaking our ego. Others say the water inside the coconut is akin to the atma, soul, and that's what we should focus on, not just the exterior idol. We should look at the essence, bhavarth, not the literal words, shabdarth.

In south India, besides breaking a coconut, a pumpkin is also cut as a symbolic sacrifice. In Tantra puja, the top of a coconut is sliced off and ghee is poured in it. It is then placed in the fire, and declared to be a Brahmin bali!

26

Puja

Have pujas been conducted since Vedic times?

In the Vedas, which are 4000 years old, yagnas are mentioned, not pujas. The word puja is 2500 years old, first found in the Griha Sutra which talks about rituals. In yagnas, there was no idol. Agni, fire, was the medium through which gods were invoked. This is called Nigam parampara, tradition, while puja is called Agam parampara. The Griha Sutra repeatedly talks about someone being pujaniya, worthy of reverence. The word puja perhaps comes from there or from south India. In Tamil, pujai or pusai means flowers, or offering of flowers, something not seen in Vedic times. As time went by, yagnas gave way to pujas. Nowadays, we don't do yagnas at all; we do their abbreviated form, which is havan.

What is the basic difference between yagna and puja?

Yagna has no idols, and is done in open air, while pujas usually have an idol and you need a temple to do them. In yagnas, agni is important, while in pujas water and flowers are important.

Water is poured over the idols—this is known as doing abhishek. However, the tatva, principle, of both is exactly the same.

What is the process of doing pujas?

There are simple and complicated pujas, but puja is similar to what you do for a guest arriving in the house. In a yagna, too, first there is avahan, or invocation, of the gods, and then bhog is offered—say, in the form of ghee—to assuage their hunger, while saying 'Swaha'. Then you ask them to give you their prasad, gift, and bid them farewell through a ritual.

The same happens in a puja. Before the avahan, you ready yourself by taking a bath, wearing fresh clothes, preparing the space where you'll invite the god. When you begin, the god is given a seat. Avahan is a ritual to breathe life into the idol, what is called pran pratishtha. After this, you treat the idol like a living entity, not an inanimate idol. A seat and footstool are given for the god to relax; he is offered water, and sometimes abhishek is done; he is given clothes and jewellery; chandan (sandalwood) is applied, and incense is lit to make the room fragrant. In the case of a god, a yogyapavit (sacred thread) is provided, and a goddess receives a mangalsutra (sacred necklace for married women). Then bhog is served. Then aarti is done with a lamp and bhajans are sung. The moment for phalastuti then arrives, where you ask for wish fulfilment and seek forgiveness for any lapses. Finally, it is time for the visarjan (immersion in water).

This is the entire process of a puja, where a transaction is essential. Sometimes the meaning of puja is lost in translation: puja is not prayer; it is an exchange. It was the same during the yagna tradition. Also, once the yagna was over and the gods had departed, the site of the yagna would be burnt, all traces of it removed. Similarly, the puja idol is immersed in water and the puja area is cleaned off to leave no signs of it. But in established temples the deity is always present, and in a sense alive, so you don't have to go through the ritual of avahan or pran pratishtha—it is different.

If we don't ask for anything, is it not called puja?

Culture, sabhyata, began with exchange; whenever two human beings meet, there has to be an exchange of some kind. How do you establish a relationship with god—that's the purpose of a puja. You offer something to god, and ask him to fulfil your wishes in return. You approach him because you have ichhas, desires. If you don't, you've become a vairagi or a tapasvi, and don't need the gods at all. Desire is not seen negatively; in a householder's life, you're bound to have them. So, a puja is the time for you to express your desires. There is, of course, no guarantee that your plea will be answered—it depends on your karma as well—but you ask god to make adjustments in their plans for you!

What is the meaning of offering bhog?

The fundamental quality of a living being is that he feels hunger. A guest is first offered water and food. The gods too have an appetite. But bhog is not only food; it can be various things from clothes to pleasant sensations—fragrance, light in the form of diyas, etc. In Nathdwara, Rajasthan, there used to be asht-chhaap kavis, poets who composed paeans to the gods; so the gods love poetry and music just as we do. Even dhyan, concentration, is offered to god, and can be considered a bhog.

When and how did the connection between puja and music develop?

In medieval times, foreign invaders from Central Asia frequently raided and destroyed temples in India. When devotees became anxious, the rishis told them that they didn't need physical temples to worship god. A mandir can be in your mind (maan ke andar). Through the medium of music, sangeet, they created inner temples. Vallabhacharya of the Shrinathji temple at Nathdwara, Rajasthan, declared that he would create mandirs through poetry, music, ragas. So there are eight pujas for each prahar, and for every prahar, there's music. While sleeping, on waking, while eating, in the evening, in summer, in winter, and so on. It's a practice developed in the fourteenth and fifteenth centuries.

So bhajans and aarti have emerged from this music?

There's a slight difference between sangeet and bhajan. Music can be descriptive, general. Bhajan or aarti has a specific purpose. Aarti is moving a lamp to see god properly. This is linked with the idea of darshan, seeing the divine. The yagna tradition focused mainly on listening to the mantra, or shruti, since there was nothing to see. When mandirs emerged, seeing god became important. In south India, where idols are often made of black stone, it's difficult to see them. So, the temple's pujari, priest, moves the lamp in front of the idol momentarily so you get just a glimpse of the idol. In the Nathdwara temple, there's a curtain, which is parted just for a brief sighting of the idol; this is called a jhanki. It is believed that if you stare at the idol for too long, you'll be spellbound and never leave the temple.

Bhajans are sung in praise of god. They describe his appearance and beauty, and demonstrate how the devotee has seen the god properly. They also talk about his greatness, tell stories about their victories over different asuras, how they saved different devotees, and so on. Sometimes, I feel that this is to teach us how to relate with others. If you go to someone's house and are not offered food or water, if nobody speaks to you, asks about your well-being, praises you, you'll feel nobody is giving you any importance.

There's a story in the Ramayana where Jambuvan, the king of bears, praises Hanuman lavishly to encourage him to cross over to Lanka and save Sita. Aarti and bhajan are somewhat like this, almost like a motivational speech you're given when you first join a company.

What is the difference between doing puja for a god at home and in a temple?

In homes, there are puja ghars, a room or an alcove where the god's idol is kept. Sometimes, temporary shrines are created for specific pujas, like for Satyanarayana or Ganesha, during festivals. In a permanent shrine like a temple, there is puja every day, morning and evening. Various rituals are performed, and there are priests. The basic difference is between temporary and permanent shrine, and there is no priest in a house; its members conduct their own puja.

Devotees believe that the owner of a house is the god who stays in it and the inhabitants are merely tenants. Gods that are invited temporarily are guests. Ultimately, a god is created by a devotee and his devotion. It is a matter of the relationship, and it's up to you how to believe in god.

What's the difference between a vrata, fasting, and a puja?

Yagnas were conducted by men; there were also pujaris of different kinds—ritwik, udgathra, etc.—who too were male. Vrata is typically for women because for a vrata, you don't need an idol or a temple. It's all in the mind, and there are no external rituals. You fast, fast without water, choose to eat certain foods—like only chana and gur for Santoshima, wake the entire night in jagaran, etc. It's all done on your own body, where your body becomes the instrument of reaching out to god. Vrata is a kind of puja done without the paraphernalia. This is tantra, where tan means body; mantra is when dhyan is involved, which is done by the mind, or mann; and yagna is when a yantra or technology is involved.